Residual Synonyms for the Name of God
Copyright 2016 by Lewis Freedman

First Edition, First Printing
Ugly Duckling Presse
232 Third Street, #E303
Brooklyn, NY 11215
uglyducklingpresse.org

Distributed in the USA by
SPD/Small Press Distribution
1341 Seventh Street
Berkeley, CA 94710
spdbooks.org

ISBN 978-1-937027-65-0

Design by Doormouse
Typeset in Baskerville
Cover printed letterpress at UDP
Printed and bound at McNaughton & Gunn
Edition of 1000
Support for this publication was provided by
the National Endowment for the Arts

RESIDUAL SYNONYMS
FOR
THE NAME OF GOD

Lewis Freedman

Ugly Duckling Presse
Brooklyn, NY

PREFACE

THEY grew attracted between two funerals, one for each of their loss. Was it the surprise of seeing yourself substituted for the one you'd felt for . . . the stability of positional roles reverberating electrically between you as, for once, a non-transcendental desire. A clear recuperation emerging from sudden disappearance, humbled in the judgment becoming both the one you lost together. So is the ghost . . . walking . . . structure in pursuit of a generationally transmitted degenerative order. If I'm a captive here by faking it, what makes it? If I'm a captain here by faking it . . . there's a robot in the ruin of the right arm stretched by legend into the wedge . . . fancy. Uh-mmmmmm . . . Uhmmmmm-hh-hh-hmmmmm . . .

THE proper treatment of subjectivity requires a symbology that repeatedly offers a special apology to the subject. There is as yet an imminent dealing with the second layer . . . paved with the sacrifice of everything for grouping which is how we recognize a structure. The left branches are masks at both levels, a floating froth to be printed in two parts: each exercising a fain to imbue life. We regret these two parts. The 91 residual names that filter through 8 attributes of God are obliterated masks that protect the old and dead like a mirror with the names and attributes of assisting vitalities. Let's put the Great Masters of Literature outside like a mirror devoted to a friend and comment on the schema of the first layer which is due to imply any moment. Each object is outside power, and as such no object is outside a system of power, and as such we regret that this work should prove its contribution.

L. Freedman.

London, 5th – 7th October, 1946.

CONTENTS

INTRODUCTION 17

RESIDUAL SYNONYMS FOR THE NAME OF GOD . . 25
1. Hype 27
2. The Source Text 28
3. Your Health 29
4. Speak Ersatz 31
5. Dean Backwards 32
6. The Choice 33
7. The Modern Combine . . . 34
8. WhoDo (remind me of a) . . . 35
9. Phyllo O Hopper 36
10. His Conceit 37
11. Print Job *or* Dream Job . . . 41
12. My Remote Accuser 42
13. Chosen Doctor in Rewrite . . . 43
14. Notes on the Passivity of Hike . . 45
15. One of the Worlds 46
16. Heaps in Hidden Places . . . 47
17. Round About Suspended *or* Spheres . . 48
18. Damn 49
19. Dear Backwards Metaphor . . . 50
20. BoBoBo in the Good Word *or* The Good Eulogy 51
21. The Elephant in the World . . . 52
22. A Model of Uniqueness . . . 53
23. The Inaccuracy of One . . . 54
24. Dude 55
25. Who Said That 56

26. Bored of Alternate Dimensions . . 57
27. What Sees Can't Be Seen By One Seeing Through It 58
28. Attachments of Old Mail . . . 59
29. The God of God Contaminated . . 60
30. Halt! Secret Song of Sheep . . . 61
31. Really High 62
32. Just Waiting 63
33. what about it? 64
34. Responsibility Beast 65
35. Courtship of the Destruction of the Whole . 66
36. Pun on Erase 67
37. A Prior Meaning of Searcher . . . 68
38. Living Business Face 69
39. Supplier of Those Words . . . 71
40. The Works 72
41. A Tone 73
42. Page of Big Mercy 75
43. The Headlong Memorial . . . 76
44. Wise Man Juniper 77
45. They Know Your Thoughts . . . 78
46. The Hand Turned Colour Through Light . 79
47. Surprisingly Every Time! . . . 80
48. Come On Fishy 81
49. Fist-e-Pure 82
50. Awkward Entrance 83
51. Epigraphic Piercings 84
52. The Plurality of the Worlds of Jacques . . 85
53. Face Rift 86
54. The Harp of Failure 87
55. Silver Animus Employee . . . 88

56. The Manifold Worlds of Lives	89
57. <u>An Answer in Writhing . . .</u>	90
58. <u>The Neighbour This Name Indicated/Touched</u>	91
59. Mank the Transportability of Relation-ing	92
60. The Worker B	93
61. World of Rex	94
62. Straight Show Now Tell Me	95
63. Like	96
64. Hoodie Up/Hoodie Down	97
65. If I Here	98
66. Consumerist	99
67. The Portation of Thought	100
68. Truth (for Corporations and Cooperatives)	101
69. A Consolation Icon for Every Sign	103
70. The Righteous Tune to Tetris	104
71. Earnings on High Risk High Yield Ventures	105
72. Whine Quality Analysis	106
73. Infinitesimal Wealths	107
74. Hymn Without Effort	108
75. Big Mane	109
76. In the Service Industry: We Who Spoke	110
77. Variance in Spectacles	111
78. A Mouldy Ology of the Monad	112
79. Privileging the Primer for Revolt	114
80. Shock Until Now	115
81. Pattern Prodigy Conversion	116
82. Carob Berekhas	117
83. Stuck in Addition	118
84. Bitter Brand	119
85. Reincarnation of Agreement	120

86. Friend?	121
87. By-Knock-You-Lars	122
88. Hyper-Rapport	124
89. Oh Heathens and Heavens	125
90. Money Wrap	126
91. A Peaceable Move	127
THE NAME	129
I. Pronunciation	129
II. Visibility	141
III. Memoir	146
ACKNOWLEDGEMENTS	156

The meaninglessness of the name of God indicates its situation in the very central point of the revelation, at the basis of which it lies. Behind every revelation of meaning in language . . . there exists this element which projects over and beyond meaning, but which in the first instance enables meaning to be given. It is this element which endows every other form of meaning, though it has no meaning itself. . . . Its radiation or sounds, which we catch, are not so much communications as appeals. . . . What the value and worth of language will be—the language from which God will have withdrawn—is the question which must be posed by those who still believe that they can hear the echo of the vanished word of the creation in the immanence of the world. This is a question to which, in our times, only the poets presumably have the answer.

— Gershom Scholem

for Arthur Marmorstein (1882-1946)
with love

INTRODUCTION

'If my cart creates a turd who speaks through a moat of filth in the human gaze . . . learn to cleave to it'. These words are quoted in the name of the failures of the old interpreters whose recourse was to photograph their own acknowledgement. These allegorists' twofold torture was just their environment softening them up to be detainees of the euphemism: 'law'. It's true . . . that these same prisoners are the guys who arrive at the media coverage with a best-books-for-any-moment test . . . but without knowledge of the whole . . . uhhh, mockumentary about real event genre. How strange . . . that thought is more concerned with shape than material! It seems, therefore, worth some amount of time (a while?) to draw nearer to conceiving the administration of the word as the editors of representative shape . . . characters themselves anticipation . . . present-day dudes on the way to class representing . . . religion-of-straight . . . by interviewing shape discomfort in . . . dedication to calling each other 'fags' in the story.

The term 'network' rightly used or not produces types of examples . . . types of examples drunk on four centuries of graves engendering each other's decay in an underground work connexion. To our thinking we are dealing with our whole lives . . . devoted to the development of attempts both serious and superficial to distort a point of reference beyond recognizable failure. One is then, rightly or wrongly, surprised by the unreadability of the meagre results planed in long rows of fogged-over battle formations. Imagine a full library of books that are overdue primarily and secondarily due to an imperfect relationship between method and application. Isn't it amazing?

If you divide the combined age of your community into seconds you can schematize thinking . . . but it's a mean task. Exactly the opposite of what I think I've gathered . . . there is scarcely a page in the following pages without at least some lines expressing the productive force of individual thought deposits. Some strike uncouthly in the climax . . . some are custom-made chronologies, polemical to the point of barely motivated . . . but also we placed our own misfortunes as quiet and unassuming tracers who teach contemporary philosophy to primitive religion . . . so . . . deep shadows are to blame? One example from page 87: 'When a person apologizes in an apologetic country, she will be treated as the material of historical method within the theme of history . . . she must be forgetting to be prepared in advance for the need to abandon arising shapes. "Papa", "Goomi" (your parents), with their/its good and bad effects, allow you your protean faculty of adaptability. The happening decline we attended in the rickety dogma shed was shaking in the formulating lung . . . altering . . . the being against belief'. How far out is this present writer's wish to sip the chafe from somatic bonds and spit it under new restrictions he doesn't understand! Four centuries of analysis . . . and thousands of reactive teachers grooving on their words as verdicts brought glistening from the fount of their fresh selves to pronounce a contribution that is to beeee thought . . . that is to be the task of the children of the world . . . and if thou delay its real meaning . . . thou shalt surely die.

You know, it's a genre convention, like surfers' hair. Enlightenment is to be thought . . . it's safer that way. Imagine an impressive ever-deepening awareness as long as it's not inferior to any other. Thanks . . . thanks to the naked advancements of Zoroaster, Buddha, Jesus, Paul, Origen, and Augustine . . . we cab our way to social functions on paved roads under the Big Scribe. Heathendom and idolatry as weapons . . . this is a teaching used by a priestly clan to restrain a lower class, assimilated by parable at the manifold points around skin.

Why is this here? Nothing sounds quite as new and original to you as your zeal to have the foreign mark diminish your individuality. This idea repeats the emerging pattern or emerges in the repeating pattern or patterns the emerging repetition or patters on the repetition of emergence. Any way you disturb it, it will burn the living instance to play you back . . . your idea of the masses turning shamefacedly into theatrical time. There were, are, and will be times when biasing the spirit of the words at this Place . . . towards an amplified and roving immortality . . . can't be overrated . . . though . . . on the whole it's never been . . . it's never been underrated . . . and we don't have to put up . . . with this . . . this frame . . . as leading arbiter of our fate . . . it's a very poor arbiter!

What does this matter? This work endeavours to effect the event by circling its preservation as having spread from its ancient sources . . . thinking its touch far into the omens and needs of our nowadays. With all the paranoia of a solitary vigil, we will administer the problems of writing and reading to the little mental conditions that have changed so over the last eighteen hundred years. 'Good to-day' the male police officer exclaimed . . . 'Thanks, Happy Christmas' replied the Minister's wife . . . this is extremely fucking disturbing . . . and bears the character of almost the same difficulties arranged in the many hundreds of cases tackled in this here folio: an airing and classification of the known and unknown searching graves . . . each losing . . . to agitate and harass the newly risen consequences of their failed methods. The medical doctor, no matter how advanced, holds the space . . . in our society . . . of eternally primitive information . . . ditto the teacher . . . which is why they're so easily seen . . . so easily hurt by this email . . . so unable to say the shifting aspect they felt lost . . . viewing instead . . . some rediscovered "gem-of-a moment" of existence.

Let's remain rewinding there remotely in 19-91 a little longer while . . . the lucidation is kicked out for its snow-like vastness. The law of this material then . . . was a series of documents too large to carry around . . . but now is a string of language too vast to read. I'm not complaining but . . . now you have to pay the slightest difference to the conceptual attention bank . . . it's unconscious . . . I mean not conscious . . . what'd you call me? Did people? Invent them? I mean, we have to weigh in the threat by habit, breaking up its narrative with just a thimble of the past and just a normal of the future, right? Also the local ignorance of the word must be never be lost sight of . . . its connotations are cultural standards which protect normalcy, its detonations are just striking events with fact estimates. For example, I say canned sardines are just one side issue . . . of an older generation who were more habituated to smelling like fish (canned laughter). While you say new and old can't be divorced from the riddle . . . missing or not . . . of the surrounding world . . . missing or . . . at least the extent of its oversimplification.

Like the furious perception of a squirrel I at once saw and thought? . . . I liked it. Therefore the same way we human feelings longed for the super-seen sloping down towards a stupid beauty that is only not an exit . . . we hoped to be reprimanded for longing for the idea in the image of the super-soaker-three-thousand which culminated meaningfully in a friend. How can we learn something about three-thousand texts without reading and airing our terminal gems? Print and prison in the agitated metavariable of a repenting mind . . . they did not contribute their proper share of vastness into the supernatural latrine . . . so a side issue neglects them redirecting their attention.

I know a harp when I see a harp that must never be lost sight of. We are here as a sucky estimate unfulfilling the temporal condition of some future riddle. And yet it is the sublimest deal the body invented . . . to begin in words a passage means a passage means it makes sense. Why release our methods to their easy justifications . . . like unsorts the shortcut to a history of names abbreviated into the spokesperson of our time whose popularity types the ill-luck of anyone. A bitter youth deer weekend discarded in the alto corners still providing the investment of magic and prayer . . . a step detected towards the entrance to all media controversy . . . at its best in a long list . . . mirage and myth and actual shore arose afterwards around the type of song . . . you know.

To counter your face try to present a strange contrast between the features on one side . . . remote centuries' contact will . . . will be clear feelings on the other. Thought thought through and through some sauce in my teether. Popular names in our Literature iterating on the warping phone until their location is precise pronunciation . . . people saying '!*??# it' to ordinary works of genius forgetting the bitter struggles they invented to become them. Later on to keep listening to the altered fix that reliance can be placed upon . . . by indirectly exposing them to be institutional attributes of personal crudities

. . . crossing some ocean side by side linked by persecution and the bits it's broken. A contest of proof in which situational and dramatic irony advances to a height in which writing becomes an internal movement . . . of the burden of great change upon movement . . . interspersing the vogue with . . . like what wine is actually going on in us.

Residual Synonyms for the Name of God

WHILE the freedom of explanation has often been investigated as agent, it is hidden: immersed in its own daylight. When we speak we travel the registry by night. Though there *is* an intra-enumeration like a bought election, the Alphabet, expected prior, seems to come later. Standing blind and feeling moss. Where's the baby? So the later collected hinders even the artifice it owes to origin. The quiet but totalizing popularity of any single digit number . . . but the number 91 as a mystical speculation would dupe us in surprise . . . it's all welded with an ancient partiality whose predilections are unknown.

Any attempt to form form doubly as a mysticism left a sense that we didn't know we were being looked for. So we compromised—no more sources—already where it was needless to look behind. Many strenuous mental struggles, often lasting centuries, politicized the first layer like phases of ignorance, phases of ignorance that keep on getting you fired, grant you refuge in sports. Some such unionized medium is concealed within these words as a growth bearing witness to a gestation fertilized by endless falling into a turn in the past which, lacking a teller, can never be paid out.

They whistled internally and externally. The cleansing assertion of a hella-beat-up acquittal, idolatrous with the material mouth of its superstition come true. Not a dying culture was dying, it was instead debating the causes of its changing, admitting genius where imperishability was sourced, and publicly/privately/religiously expressing the inefficiency of public transportations. Surely we need to boycott any service areas bearing on the manifold entitlements of disabling event.

Even if one were born automatically as in the legend, no searcher could pass unnoticed by the question of the bargain which works on age . . . no one could step down with a brick and teach that brick to nurse her back to health.

Our list gives 91 names. Each name in the catalogue must learn to understand that it is no human. But technically it is. Or it may appear that way to any animal full of error, correct by law. I am talking about the human research apparatus. My acceptance/attitude/screaming is alphabetical, is arranged in an alphabetical order, is chronological, engraves sexual experience to gain identity, is frequently lost in its boundaries, experiences loss of identity through sexual experience. He only thinks he's screaming his own relationship to possession. This will be dealt in the following catalogue.

(1) Hype

Why this searching (or not) is wrong occurs almost in one of the very oldest parts . . . a consensus of whales laying down the elemental stipulations at the beginning of world . . . and also here in this bung instant. Its designation the mirage of an exclusively unlocked language . . . it just happens to get put together sick before the music. Didn't just do it in old . . . new think twice about . . . inclining high to see three young ravens feeding from the sun stopped still for that escape. Where is a dose of the kid-mind we find in I opening a crisis in both schools? Save for the mail order bribe by words . . . or bind me with quickening cash heeded anger . . . it's a right community pillar to the throat . . . opposed to a kind of singing where the voice stretches up the spine to the crest of the skull and down while rising from the belly.

(2) The Source Text

This could be shortened to Sex and is used very frequently, especially to denote a man's marking of his physical relation to texts or sources. The alphabet is a passage used to speed up this testimonial record. We reveal our plans for a useless society to the heart and deeds of the rubric . . . group to get some teleological baseline . . . not for proof of evidentiary intention but to use immediately in the parable. We learned the idea of doing anything from some annoying joke within the culture. This parable is very often repeated at the partition of responsibilities . . . between seer and artist. Great is . . . the power of the seer . . . national animals crowded inside the shorthand of perception . . . tired electronics playing some beautiful teaching beyond the homilist's dare. Fault timed the crowd divides Harry Potter higher than its creator . . . harmed in the corollary willful rules of some removed level . . . put playing ground.

(3) Your Health

One of the most usual poses to bear soluble time through the sentences, I consistently assert like I begin in some counterpart of loss that's anything other than begotten plot . . . far be it from me meets the mail thing with miles to shore. The dispute is age arranging the face at what is recognized as surface . . . trying . . . to find fault with the millions of your replenishing . . . directed against those who found fault with the left memory scribbles replaying: one to cheat for five. I'm accusing a title of having created worlds that slander the memory of the serpent's (or 'duration hose's) famous saying. He found he was ready to make all the trees place a double bearing in the stolen mind . . . very often now the indistinguishable is anonymously the sane. I see this sermon staring at the surface of the pho. What do ye want with food? Go and title a trouble for your contemporaries . . . supplying you with moves on their antennas' behalves. Evidence: gadfly to the maxim . . . evidence the failings of the maxim to supply more than an implied politics for its abundantly mangled severity supply. Surely this is directed together with an erasure in the present: stir up my honour . . . before my honour . . . my honour is nothing . . . before the honour of my honour. Descending in the dialogue there to be magnified . . . Rat 1: I'm which I try to remain . . . to anticipate . . . the real . . . is not in agony it is agony . . . Tim: I'm quoting the inducing team here . . . if I went with them . . . what good can I be . . . to them . . . beguiled by notice of a spark . . . I'm like . . . is this an official spark . . . you can tell . . . if the speaking at the edges is louder than the gut . . . Top: Leave him alone . . . he's like a scribe who didn't rise early to go to the roof alone . . . and engage in the dilemma of being . . . trapped first in meeting . . . sky in the difference between . . . living on a roof and jumping off a roof . . . and now he wants to be punished.

(4) Speak Ersatz

A known punishment is the loss of your soul . . . but did you know . . . like the national scene resists the foreign language speaker . . . great wealth passively corrects its crime by making pubic hair iridescently visible . . . through cloth . . . as a metaphor for . . . the negation of the said?

(5) Dean Backwards

A cookie for the wrong judge . . . a cookie substituted for the wrong meal and cursed all those who translated the shake. We find it threatening. This is in agreement with a constitutional rule. To stop only when you deny the implicitness of your generation by saying, 'There is neither judgement nor judge' to emphasize, 'Yes, there is judgement, and there is judgeship, and it is encroaching, thinking in categories, to a summary place'. At length in a following . . . a stencil repeats, 'There is a judgement, and it is accusatory, and each person shall be judged individually'. It's a malfunctioning cloud . . . drifting for a doctrinaire machine . . . in the important electrical lifeline-lined sky. How closely we are allied to its aspect of not getting us . . . to the reward bereaving in the name of suffering punishment . . . to a source of not watching in the question of cause.

(6) The Choice

Quote high school end quote. Four years of almost incomprehensible warnings and rebukes from conceited self-martyrs who probably couldn't have known better. At least we ourselves were a demon-inspired range of malevolent holiness . . . we felt at the centre of that recording compound and circumvented ourselves with the marks of our own newals of incomprehensibility. Form next to think of the sensual imagery that continued well beyond the presupposed waiting for conversion. There is, I suppose, a good historical reason for thinking the associative method of restriction benevolent and liberatory . . . like what the fuck listened in . . . an erased greatness of unsatisfactory possibilities. Changes . . . circles spinning the ingestion of bad food through yesterday's fixation . . . a simile chastised by distress for taking the long cure . . . when my own weakness is applied fullness unable to relate to unity. Yes, it's a place matter of cork floating on the water table . . . as itself experiencing a predictive incubation . . . to formulate a to cross a field away . . . very blurring the parade . . . as though the drought could be dismissed out of hand which, of all your limbs, dangled an encolpion for protection. In spite of this consciousness of healing by neglect . . . this virtual portico of bringing it back home . . . none of this can be led astray. The image of mice being led by some god-sent who's only trying to escape them . . . who cries out in its desire to be rejected the very examples its teacher gave . . . for though we weren't then wearing our attention . . . we were touching up that sympathetic magic . . . you know, the problem of mimesis in philosophy is that it really can't be rejected.

(7) The Modern Combine

When your ego feels crowded by all the biographical reasoning . . . it is uniquely in order to serve you as the wise rearrangement of place! The bad guest insists on the payoff being grateful for every trouble afforded her. There can be no doubt so you photocopy the try to write Twitter's gnostic datascape without irony. This may be kind of nuanced see . . . blasphemed by the shortness of the day, the at-best sluggishness of the highlights' task, the boring urge of sound boxing, and the popularity of the rival factory . . . just as in the prehensile screws of an individual's moment, persona figures in reverse. Two cows . . . sensitively contributing a knot . . . one is facing enchantment, the other: commodity status . . . upon which should we place the yoke? On the illustration so similar it is mistaken . . . and must admit . . . if it were to be really hard on itself . . . that yes it is a sociopath. What it depicts is the parable of the orphan who was brought up on a ladder. Whenever he would wave goodbye he would boast about the control and security of his footholds. If someone below were fainting he would draw a pail of water from the wooden rungs and rouse them. He would hew real wages from the connections he found companionable about the stringers. But the real narrative was found kept in the world to come. Unable to tolerate the difference between doors closed and almost closed, a bottle was placed in a combat boot 500 times before any piece of continuance was caught. The gist of this piece was pathological, a paranoia to reinterpret desire as though it were a thief whose psychic condition is being reprimanded counting. Requiring these supporting details because any one case is unwillable, finally, the authentic can't get over the piles of preserves.

(8) WhoDo (remind me of a)

In several simple platform sayings . . . being too clean to require other explanation or designation . . . a silence surrounds these often-repeated sayings . . . like a religiously-valued bomb that performs miracles . . . which don't require praise . . . which show Pythagoras a dinosaur . . . mixed-up butthead standing backwards at the zombie apocalypse . . . adopting the source from passing materials . . . I am keeping a peaceful decorum . . . very peaceful as the core expands to include its big pear.

(9) Phyllo O Hopper

By the way . . . an anagrammatic order enters the acts reproduced here . . . the actual words of the contemporary sound here to utter irreducibility . . . possibly end in all things. Outta Khilta. An agricultural invention of both incubatory sleep and graphic dream-epiphanies. Then back to a discussion of this surface re-invigorated by the lowly logon who veils the pre-original.

(10) His Conceit

It is a well-established fact that there is nothing in the word common . . . it was not used to a predictable impact . . . so it overlapped in quotation as usage. That this innovation be regarded as measured gland by when it was introduced. A reformed forté in the dawn of a remarkable day naming the shroud you are sitting in . . . carries with it the visual apprehension of a slight opening to a broad mass of antiquity. You were right to regard this as momentous, you were right to deny it. The history is never the starting point . . . the malady is never having thought . . . who appealed to a theme to survive context . . . who symbolized home to reload a pact with culture? The cancellation isn't sufficient, the term is outplayed by needs: the purer astrology of language. We have already seen that the fight for retention is in spite changed places. So too, just because you can destroy something as instinct doesn't mean you get a clearer idea of what is not known to us. Examine the struggle you hear in the voice of this work: in Literature, they used it as a combatant to the documentary conclusion, but in profane-heathen mode they used it as a dialogic passage to mediate paradox as resistance . . . tó aid the step away transformed in performance to a required oath-grammar neither within nor without the Absolute Realty Company. No wonder the elimination round treats us like resisted confession . . . I want to point out the favored cyborg in the conclusion circle . . . caution the strangers . . . but won't risk the significance of the exorcism . . . correction won't risk a scene at the exorcism.

(a) Babies for Idols

A dearth of explanation in the anti-if of creative toll. If it read that H & E were agreeable Godheads, what is the cart sonar? The eonic foreknowledge of a sweltering moon before it is subsumed to invisibility by a sun . . . a photography all scrolled out for the Museum of Committees . . . speechifying the architecture of the . . . If we can transcend a live broadcast in synthetic experience. I really like your phase of applications . . . this got an angle to catalyze the bind . . . may be gathered by reenactment of arousal . . . our problem is that our problem is an apprentice to the vogue. Or how consistent is the strange . . . is its discussion attached to the parallel arrangement of a discussion objecting altogether to removing the mandala from the memorial? We refuge to talk a transient shop shown later if not meaning. May the avoidance of our names make His paranoia tolerable.

(b) The Name Right in Front of You

A conspiracy is what we typically urge towards in dialogue . . . it is custom to suggest that purpose obscures a set of facts that links persons to organizations in a farcical arrangement of proof. In every mention of this system parallel texts are assumed everywhere . . . to be found. When it tastes like chicken . . . they used to say . . . proverbs are never too late.

(c) The Mojo to Get Carried Away

We saw angels kicking it . . . a can further away than you can . . . designated to hear the boat when there are no words . . .

there are words. There are worlds in many places to scan . . . prominent individuals for their further meaning . . . owing to the manifold protectcia papered to word the doubt so it sounds a lot like you. The doubt arose from the intention of the other side to swerve as necessary, link all of the links, be shown a yet to be implicated space, bring down the three men who killed him, patent the stand-in, marginalize the species, &c.

(d) The Use of an Oath in Deliberate Error

Of the many instances in the duration of this recognition we refer directly to the connection between oath and the development of contemporary states. We've never found or doubted the instrument by which the following generation always used it . . . a careful investigation shows the weirdest game is the game of the correct or the true . . . and we refute both the refutation of and the far-reaching theories based on it. The form or matter out of which the first of all kisses was based is the object to be used greeting the coming into appearance in a greeting. When administered to a cadaver we note the repetitious pursuit of presence. When my father used to enter or leave the house he would shout, 'all appearances are striking empty against the being responsible' . . . it got so it was casually specific for me. When my father would pray I would be forced into guessing which crisis was contemporaneous with him, which older, which was omitted by his copyists, which was inaccurate to his son, and which crisis was also poesis. Please. Not as we read . . . the words are omitted as a real basis for example . . . in the time of the answer the same is the case . . . as in the age of the theory. Do you experience aloneness . . . as the gathering before construction . . . as a feasible misunderstanding? Brought up as a formulary in the ancient storage time . . . some path of document interlocks the reading of this to a loss of control older than that formulary . . . but before . . . the show itself.

(11) Print Job or *Dream Job*

In an old volatile mustachio . . . planet collage for protein issue must suffice. Appearance compelled to use Miranda's right approach to the value of good . . . confessing at the interview . . . how we've never revealed a friend's secret . . . see, loyalty, I am loyal to a fault . . . when asked to voice our biggest weakness. Counter-argument: they don't deal with cosmogony until after competition, derivation, of course budget, so the situation now is a need-all notion of concealment . . . like all lofty notions of concealment please come to the front . . . or all y'all who don't know how to swim no good . . . contrite and humble in spirit . . . make your precautionary exit. There's too much information on the ladder . . . too much vice and pride to really scale it. Who says meditation must involve a suppression of the ego . . . out there on the court trying not to feel pride if it hits . . . loss when it misses . . . all versed up on the stupid Salinger frequency . . . American beauties like ourself . . . tuned into navigate the haughties show.

(12) My Remote Accuser

Every reader first imitates a human being . . . and about these severed risks . . . an outside force earlier than saying. Do you think it's encouraged by the Day of Judgement? I think it likes a barb . . . a just war for want of helen rebuked . . . any chastisement other than any old to relocate the stank and shit of experience. Look up . . . the immediate plan for epiphany . . . a faint sign eliminated in the bowelled what . . . a play accuser eliminates wow parallel to wow in patience range, weaving boll-weevil through the historical name of brought you up. In the shine of a lentil . . . cramming so hard . . . to see the infinite in a polished fold . . .

(13) Chosen Doctor in Rewrite

No basis for assuming the slightest ground for sectioning . . . similar to information. Before it does not appear in the circular drawer . . . the joke was perfectly aware even before it added the work ethic part . . . and so can't be an original. You are like a son who complies with all his father's requests . . . you are like the great pacifist who endears himself to peace in a time of war. Spreading uses onto words like a peacemealer feeds the same stones daily at the altar of the law . . . you can expand your pupils to grasp seeing. The sad fact saying it deserves it in the passing attention. A certain onus in sure thought . . . the same passage furnishing the corrupt materials of an inner life . . . informers . . . confiscating the boom boom increasing and decreasing the sad inner life changes. I got miles of barbed wire with the words and a human skull endeavouring to depict a wing prohibited by the law . . . not to scroll while reading. As if a blot of a book may be drawn upon to express the discrepancy between the same sentence written or said. In the legend . . . the whole world is a ceremony limited to letting the rain come down and this presumably purifies you. Who is comforting the old woman seeking to be an intermediary magician? After an intermediary is discussed . . . a further chapter devoted to frequencies detected in an age of reason. Why not just have a big paycheck descending once a year? With the same words used to condition the lament . . . the idea kind of wears the causes into turns . . . our teacher mixes the days in a reflector. Why? To crucify light in the way of the will . . . to persecute the Lions in the second half . . . the second half is required to owe the victory to will. The familiar abundance of longing in the third and fourth quarters . . . a peroration explaining a father in the voice . . . not ashamed to interpret torture. To tell you by now we anonymously show what we think . . . a number for our purposes. Points to the lived the telling and produces a figure for application. The confusion of a language that cannot separate categorization from living . . . confession . . . what might it mean if there's no mercy in the stocking? We take it to mean . . . the given verb taken to the bath is nuts. This sentence was inserted in order to avoid any confusion of the verb as regards to distinguishing pseudo-rights from pseudo-privileges . . . these underlined words are here again put as commentary to an otherwise difficult conclusion which preserves a saying omitted in the original text which reads 'variants in the corrected reading should perhaps be preserved instead of the above.'

(14) Notes on the Passivity of Hike

Correct is what they shall be afraid of . . . what's not said but that will but what will be explained. The height made visible he was afraid of heights . . . on behalf of destruction . . . any speed can be destroyed. So the national deity was kind of flattered by the eulogy we provided . . . and later we were scrutinizing around in the cemetery . . . so what? 'Fools', the stranger said, 'the dead nationalisms are buried in the cemetery of the living . . . so look there'. 'Asshole', we replied, 'those living people you're talking about are some of my besties'. After all, like God, there're a lot of people outlive the known publication of their work. Not a start or perish . . . but the name could keep an arch functioning . . . leveled visible under the blanket like a reading light.

(15) One of the Worlds

One of the worlds is explained as a goody try on some omni-shoulder. One of the worlds is teaching rain to cant through depth. She sits me up to observe the difficult doctrine of presence as meaningless. It's no wonder God's presence is everywhere shown up . . . corrected by a great catch in the text of crossing a banquet. No middle lasts in the corroborated live feed action. A long climb to the funeral of another older reading . . . order to cancel where it is . . . in a bounce delay obviated by the mingled tense scratch.

(16) Heaps in Hidden Places

Let's explain the job. The eye waits for contact . . . uncomfortably cleanses in the bluish enamel of twilight . . . as though what visitation will come to a similar opinion . . . one whose face is disguised in the lens of a watchdog. Under this watching tentacles watching . . . a body is diminished as tacky apparatus and goes and sits in trial . . . gulp. Sits and waits for twilight of the timed pane . . . serious dot so small . . . where dissolution is appointed as danger . . . the eye is an adult, right? Yeah, and the evening's a point meant to watch itself made known in tensions. It's like the associates meeting you . . . went to it in language. Later, at an informal reception it was saying the letter . . . never touches the word . . . even . . . even letters as tools to point a word's existing form . . . even in its hidden phases.

(17) Round About Suspended or *Spheres*

A pledge right under her shoe she directs. Two incredible hulks of bundled thorns donated in love and he returned the same. If finally, our discolouration was a septic re-echo of one of them dignitaries of guidance . . . forced to refute your skeptical ass with their pledges to get it right belly up with media reference . . . and you saying you can't do the work . . . the sun is sick . . . human power cord, &c. . . . Well, doubt deposits a modicum of arrows into reading head . . . but never shorts the trappings of taste. Live on our 64" flat-screen TV . . . I thought I would.

(18) Damn

The oft-repeated sin . . . stratum of excessive fatigue copying again in thought from the thought of fallen asleep within the overripe dream. Or a ring of half-anthropomorphic outsides painting the backdrop of what proves to be approaching . . . distance within the wire garnished with pictures of between telephone poles silhouetted as meaning. Some warmth ebbing from later to bear out our theory. This is also to be cooped up where the coating occurs . . . or found on the prowl as contours only of this flesh committed or sentenced to thought. That this external literature should trivially insist on a right text to dogmatically sanction the private change as already agreed upon . . . to cut a figure of this view unfolding in the water's corner . . . represents the designation of a coda-box . . . as I gather it . . . let us imagine snows regularly against a disproportionately shifting half . . . comparing an older sentence reshaped in the teaching of this . . . be half of . . . the omitted half of . . . what metaphor.

(19) Dear Backwards Metaphor

For we that is called by means of the grandparent's cooption of the grandkid. For we turn, therefore, and then . . . pledges we pass by pausing . . . grinning spiratorially to prove or disprove the usual is antiquated. It makes us found considering whether what's been to us called before was not influenced by the development of the accent I bought at the scene term . . . each slogan with its echo to declare it. We were singles when we first thought fame could redeem by having been foretold . . . judgement sentenced to surge nakedly towards its apotheosis . . . helping nobody . . . uncovering nobodies as the passage receives its tyrannical affect. But a bad thought is not regarded as a deed, right? . . . rather it dwells in that limitless unbridled expressive realm of no rendering . . . as the password-protected obelisk of contemplation evaporating . . . until one day it will bear itself at the centre of your city unaltered. Do you mean it's true . . . striking . . . a hunter's head in a barrel equals names of heads as a barrel?

(20) BoBoBo in the Good Word or *The Good Eulogy*

Virtues and crimes . . . virtues and crimes . . . no. Among the numbers that appear on the parable that inhabits our statue . . . I don't know which to choose. Hello little finger . . . we connect . . . I choose great grief. I know-I know-I know . . . I know-that-the-sufferings-are-seeeeee-through . . . I know-I know-I know . . . enveloping the brain I didn't know. A movie expresses this aspect longest, akin to a vicarious safekeeping, it never seems to stop . . . double homily pinning all the pikes onto difficulties inside of health in a remorseless eradicating of the recompense to substitute as wonder. Our latest psychic trance measure of moving house in the higher 80s. Feels good to decide from you that it did . . . this received submissive identification standing graveside of what eats fire in the statement . . . my interpretation . . . ten times nothing to write . . . the once untroubled relation . . . chicken in a bottle to be carried out. This so called spontaneous grouping things so called . . . spans delay thought I actually did write out . . . staid and stays . . . like tries and trued. It bids on remembering . . . Wayne . . . at 0176 . . . 76 . . . 383 . . . 332 . . . my birth rate makes me . . . remarkable . . . the tune occurs more so over being . . . prevailing circus it is now . . . suffering . . . in a saying segment saying . . . stinguished at last . . . a good thing, I will start with thee . . . that thou bringest the hinge . . . on living this way . . . over.

(21) The Elephant in the World

The forward-thought person would never weirdly allegorize a serpent. Why? Because she's trying to turn without writing and her mind is burping verbs, whispering disconnection disconnection against its creatored. The chief friend to constructing identity isn't a home but . . . ummm . . . a second pass . . . where there's so precisely . . . lenient . . . um, cropping . . . to extend inclination . . . inclination . . . not the inclination to forgive. Like if you trust your trans-sailor built friend, God's real person perspective will never forgive them.

(22) A Model of Uniqueness

We met Psycho in a saying . . . preached and driven into . . . fetishized denial. Until they was sacrificed to be called a catalyst . . . we were the premise eulogized . . . unable to build the cycle of public buildings. It's the policy on scale that becomes perpetuous . . . and lies behind the presentation of a stupid key to the city. Visitors repeat yourself . . . know the rule . . . this is how to intervene . . . first it is different, then it is praised. Is this the knock on nation: that it fosters a battle in the pure no help? If we'd punch in an airport uniquely renovated to deemphasize its hardwired boundaries . . . we'd find answers to questions like: is democratic space necessarily gendered? can one really go blind by looking at the sun? This our communal slavery is kneedeep in exhaustion . . . yet still we find time for police work . . . the stable boy arrested on evidence of a fine comb. This night, I say, is different . . . from all previous exaggerations of the ambulance chase scene . . . it is that to which we owe direct historical reference. For ours is the age of conclusive identification through agreement . . . stretched true by a light humiliation that cuts us from more bigger losses.

(23) The Inaccuracy of One

Popular with yourself in your hermetic room . . . monad of the case . . . case from which you threw the screen in enmity to save yourself from your own advertisement of yourself to yourself in each screen you forced yourself clear at to . . . from within which with pitiless filing you blotted to beyond doubt . . . this name is not entirely phonetic. This name occurs because it's like clear. Your throat is not now alone some . . . see swish in the herd which means . . . Peepers and Strokey on two sides of the glass, the noises denying the surface of the exposition. The so-called anonymous enumeration considers every name in order . . . to make peace among concepts . . . whose names found labour in the same catalogue . . . sharing the archaic swarms there with displaced creatures of language . . . ex-communicated . . . because they sinned about the culture's context . . . which perceives every occurrence . . . but first words. Speaking of correspondences . . . strange blizzards . . . in whose three-dimensional index . . . you're thought.

(24) Dude

When he died his nephew addressed his funeral address into his prosthetic vag based on the phrase, 'leaving, the object is the only thing delivered, suddenly ascribed from its usage'. He put himself at the mercy of the object whose placement he removed from their mist. Gone down to the garden thing, to the beds of spices which can save him, to feed in the question of the garden and gather a context for his mercy. It makes us sick.

(25) Who Said That

The captain of poetry must exist on that road . . . outside of thinking-writing. It's in some one (weighs) similar . . . to a piety's attempt to tribute divine imitation by criminalizing its own nocturnal emissions. Heaven must be the only place where a published book can be fully read . . . and I really won't condemn a book until I've read it aloud in heaven. This sounds like you heard the words . . . as underhanded tosser . . . riddles where are we. How dud we acquire this container of its own meaning? The same detrimental answers . . . by suffering! or by great happiness. The same names my composition had specified . . . in relief . . . now in disputation cause. If the cycle is to be transcended only where . . . the act in actual is chaste around its opposite . . . how often is suppressed in favor . . . of the clothing speaker's veiled spite habit.

(26) Bored of Alternate Dimensions

In discussion of addressing vice as album cover . . . the text embedded no attention to either cultural meaning or belatedness . . . erasing instead with the remark that the most unlikely thing is the really important thing. Correct like correction is the rearrangeability of the contention of the thing like content . . . like if we left the tracks on their sex frequency the content would distinguish some personal history . . . like standing drunk and seeing the drink right through to its cup. It's not a problem it's an awareness that didn't coarse . . . its path designed to be certain to be seen by the question of reading . . . since machine of human writing is machine of history . . . so our only comfort is it can't be seen.

(27) What Sees Can't Be Seen By One Seeing Through It

A blind man says to the physics of this trope . . . charred off, waits in the sun but can't get hot . . . a tacky boa bullwhip awaits my apology. It's up to you son . . . the consummate showing as chaperone to show you up . . . laid chrome applied to the light sulk by a boss you can see, for instance, only in comparison. I can't get it . . . whose stuffed shirt is this soul ironied on . . . in a bath forget it. See also the parallel story of the blind man trope appeasing the virtual of this name.

(28) Attachments of Old Mail

The visual verity this no one is surprised by. Bored shitless of the word seen . . . on the marking effect . . . by the wall. Being to space . . . travels into a cosmonautology shown later . . . to be . . . further exacting the ol' book's fit. Quicker than building . . . more ultraviolet than preserved . . . the omni-dome of the future is not only an environmentalist's playground . . . but a way to enter the present in the frequency it passes to its grave. Ok, so we embezzled the monetary gains of 'lost time' in the past . . . and is that it? . . . is our plan now really an anthology of the not yet familiar? As vice-commentator of both my own emotional response and self-forgetfulness, I am totally not aware of this. Perhaps instead, I took the money on a move whose continuance was not as inevitable as its appearance . . . so now it appears to fix or abandon a tone so . . . swathed or swabbed in its changing. Look the way the line lines up the direction of entrance with reference to the two parts of its realism: 1) meaning (I'm like that so you are too) and 2) the audially/visually bus it charged commentary charged l_mao@ thought . . . thought being eternal deferment of driving to deea beecken one weekend soon.

(29) The God of God Contaminated

What I will call 'contrary-culture' appears exorcistically most projected in what? I saw a young girl gathering the hoofs of horses as they ran . . . without fear and without any epidermal contact. I called her agent like eighteen times before she answered . . . her performance was about the disgust of touching I was told . . . about mastering the taboo of nausea . . . it was called 'the faithful shepherd' and was informed by an obscure magic called 'entangled dissent'. Now a few instances which will sufficiently packet from the recovered share of whatever *that* was. What we flattened to consider wise, violent, enigmatic, touching . . . when so praised . . . even in the ceremonial climax of immense variation . . . was, in fact, quoting itself, its own well-known antithesis . . . cruel, thinned out, engulfed, and foolish. I write the vow on the looking horn—in a closed system it's impossible to break the law. It's not unsettling that it won't reveal a secret . . . two predatory positions as the space between a shadowy awareness and its apostle . . . is what claims to having been excommunicated. I guarantee you the copier will break . . . but in order to witness this copying out . . . we must deploy it relentlessly in the same system as before . . . this the real movement of faith. In the beginning the introduction permitted us to sermonize language as event. But we find it's grafted onto an antecedent line ('the mind is in the said') and terms of the repeated are repeatedly only motives.

(30) Halt! Secret Song of Sheep

It's doubtful this can be recorded as a name. I mean if a name could occur only once (some fake Igitur) and it means the secret cart blasted from a wide angle to be mingled in our purposeful choreography . . . ? It's a revelation on parole at the unconcealed point of regarding creation. It's all parries and no parable . . . so your venomous adversary still profits from history in a previous feckin blow to the soul proprietor of this so-called riot. But no worries . . . the real meaning of this name or not is contained in a cylindrically shifting glow of the mammalian face . . . (that face which stops us in the hike up sleeve league to ask if we should wait for it to pass or walk around it) . . . mostly benign when we see it caught . . . but nipping like water-glue when it emits the phosphorescent units which supply our day-to-day-to-day . . . working a musical wind into the regularity we are bound to become like.

(31) Really High

This completely unnecessary name is generally used to signify that nothing happens. As long as we don't fall and break our sight below the possible is decreed from above: 'actualize your work plan by repeating and enlarging all of these names in the same sense' . . . another, possibly later, version reads . . . 'actualize your work plan so well it goes like the coindecision of marking expectation off, when the bird is caught by the fowler, for bird and fowler alike in their reels of bodily consents' . . . the change appears as noteworthy. Nothing further happens under the earth or within the anti-structures of unconscious unless it is bargained with . . . not Bob Marley the invalid hero . . . but the Marley that cruises the hurried turf of tragedy whispering aim like he's testing some fingernail for the shape of its future filings or tube sock for the cotton around its stretch. The face is wrong info . . . it can teach us only the sentence of the face . . . some rolodexical procession of the day . . . seconds . . . the relay speech to rush my feeling frame as report or avoid or weaken the prose of doped-up expressionism. Thirdly, it stands . . . entry beads swept aside and duddilly returning theme . . . to kiss the tone dead connexion with an ace on high . . . and all that I see is based and thought on a jonesing to be as cope in the inner drowning . . . nevermind now the malls you were commanded to visit stowing flowers up the nothing happens.

(32) Just Waiting

The spokes on this designation . . . just waiting . . . raised over nothing but . . . that info to see the pulse . . . impishly sarcastic . . . sown into post-belief foster pockets. And the greatest guest editor to be addressed in this way . . . seeping the groan up . . . problems with the idea of great is bound to err and stumble . . . ceasing immediately to be the greatest change we can observe. Just blood the gaps' appropriateness in the list of these guys' bloopers. Still I got problems with them frowning at description of my choices. If I've any need to attack a revelation at the twist-point . . . I just remind myself that angels were created approximately a thousand years before the universe . . . which enables me to dial it in . . . and throws a welcome light on why I'm getting drunk . . . swearing officer . . . it's my speech that's slurs my walk. Only after it slipped sideways did this need deserve a more detailed description. For when we witness the strain masked in directly the refuse . . . all and each manifests as forgetfulness and simulated coherency. Propaganda belittling our storage of current . . . a homemade coca-cola we whipped into foam . . . our only response our insistence on naming the replies.

(33) what about it?

Or what acts are confederate with the No Means of Repeating Proficiency? Damned if I know . . . because knowing's got the power . . . mashing its own supremacy . . . self-corroborating . . . reconciled with aesthetic of neo-hoodoo . . . which now traces the racistly-suppressed teaching that we are able duly to express a greatness and risk fortune amidst the inauspicious accusative harms of our conceited enemies . . . strange . . . that's not the power I once knew of it. Yet I might presuppose that I'm the one holding a fail . . . one of those who existed only to pretend to do so . . . and I'm not shattered by this . . . because I . . . I don't understand it. Gently gently we scatter the sordidness of our dissolving . . . the bitter omniscience of the swallows of mind. If all the trees were ink, we say, and if all the withered parchments were pens . . . we hold the nail in our dream but are too virtuous to hammer it awake. It's as though our biological foster parents' turbid siege of love could, for us, only signify sorrow. So, following our performance of the deficiency of the whole earth . . . we entered the big city . . . sat on a providential wall . . . and developed our expectation of unfortune.

(34) Responsibility Beast

The efficacy of planning is responsible for the brevity of my explanation of this subject. The chief idea is, however, a plan for expanding research to include both debt and credit. When the worst debtor is applied to light a white paper room hardens . . . its brief width and length now immutably close to her or him. So far as I can see clearly and keep in mind this still . . . requires a virtual pit of hopeless excuses . . . for the mirror which the creditor congregates at her or his reproach . . . can touch the turmoil into spin or mist and divert that very large lead to draw us homer. They dream of killing snakes . . . they dream of prosperity. They dream of a stupor brought about by anxiety . . . they dream of a profit made from drought. The individual, uttering the well-established inefficacy of despair, hears a voice of the same time and knows their type is confirmed.

(35) Courtship of the Destruction of the Whole

How do you understand the orangeness of the fire escape as the following statement: 'surviving occurs in the saying'? Answer: By the advance given . . . by the rewards of automatic inconclusive response . . . says a crap job pays very well . . . if the company emblem is furnished lion, deer, eagle, or leopard . . . all on a profane condition . . . no causal difference between presumptuous and unconscious actions. Is this all some magical punishment as one night defects its shadow in the fucking cleanliness of fear? Each grievous account just feet and pants looking down to the knocked-out actor waking back from anonymous container into fame? This all deposit, not in the least attractive, is technically instructive indeed . . . extending saying to a not all hollowed out cold and colder invisibility . . . leaving (by) only enumeration . . . to gather in a mist of its removal.

(36) Pun on Erase

Obfuscatory, but constantly discussed in. Some see its influence as a third drain which occurs so frequently it eats sinks and traces no trace. Where we care for its origin . . . its origin is very late. Its origin is always very late . . . no retroactive halving stays out later . . . it is always very late. Our investigations show it was very late in the cultic literature of the first century . . . far ahead of its time . . . virtually photographic in its material future. We know with tentative certainty (certainty as small as it is garish) that just as we sat there . . . Americans ordering Scandinavian yogurt for dessert . . . thinking we had far outdated our date . . . a displaced redaction just robo-rated a point in change and some disappearance in time started messing shit up. Neither equivalence nor growth can get used to guess thought . . . to guest thought . . . to guessed thought . . . back to change its past use. Next ailment . . . the left pant leg . . . which can be traced back to the authority of the right. A call to replace the judge's report with the meanings pondered in the defendant's examination of it . . . but for our purposes it is sufficient to point out that in the literature of the thirteenth century b.c.e., when the fur you wore still throbbed with favors (its torques out both done by and according to others), when a translator's thought could still deny the use of an original text, it feels our duty to remind you, rather than defend or explain the remainder in this use bout, that origin was already too late not to be money or sanity or the last decade or material or immaterial . . . that which denies the son he had, now emigrated to Ontario . . . he who stays indoors to deny the Ontario sun . . . and stands generally for an intention according to opposite's intended result. Oldest strata of that notice to preserve some undone frequency in the wide forgetting.

(37) A Prior Meaning of Searcher

To whom will use this disempowerment in reply . . . as in waste of line I think we're supposed to . . . do I not know that I'm the agent of the searcher we don't know? Owing to the harm we are done shackles . . . holding gold in front of the pawn shop but never getting what we want. We are weeping by analogy only . . . which complicates speech. Someone tests your friendship by trying to help you . . . because they don't know what you think and can't hold that dark corner curtailing their own appearance. Who needs this? . . . but to murder an unseen world for sounding like your name . . . because you're eager to slaughter a bent exitlessness, eager to withdraw to a silent empire of purer habit? Was this not issued so frequently as a belated question that its use changed . . . to a contribution towards consent between executor and reorderer of shall I do project? We are addicts of material progress . . . we have a need for information as meant for following . . . and we expect our struggles to come to profit.

(38) Living Business Face

In the story we graft . . . order closing out of the nasty mouth. Three years lasted . . . the hope it wasn't gonna be alright . . . witness count decreasing with repeated viewing . . . suffering taking sides: either the original has been removed or abbreviated into a more original form . . . empire dispersing the dispute as opinion. But within the city some nutshell sums up a crucifix for unthought . . . fragments letter a testament to external memory . . . substituting song for physically subsisting . . . besides . . . the source taking its first text is punished with ninety more for the fertile encouragement of our applause: denser : augur : prosterity : dinner shampoo : thing-thing : interweaver : check-off : progeny : anti-feces : bold mood : beets dear : type o' hat : clean flu : more hours please : reads the sentence : the gaffer : lee dorsey : lighthouse's rules : hands on desk : red fleece : dissections : 16th century habits : lift fork : regal lint : web sightings : flabbery : lists of pros : my secret mortgage : familial swarm : they were fronting : physical address : spinal cords and taps : recounting : a species not person : straight up flight : metaphorical heart : containing stork : geraldo rivers & joan rivera : tire siphons : girdles by another name : for micah : _ns : a golden globe : lev : pronounced posselcue : college observatory : all tithed out : of added time : tye-dye baby : omyg : classic warden : ghosted in to space : letters per missive : both boots : libel to freak : frum within : it's not a tuba : embossed : felt tip : command deer : sign on the door says : faun all : dignan : diamonds on the moles : a running race : gel in cricket : monster roving tuning party

: bees? beads? : real posh-pish : in the time of : woven tissue : impresssionario : the diamond noodle : infantaclaus : take an option : outtakes or bloopers : pinpad : vivian (riding) jackson : pillow stave : veviv : strong porter : appli-won't : geriatric aid : vinnie 'the microbiologist' thompson : wi five : original seven : marred core : in the phone : weather inside : strychnine or asinine . . . this for repeating. Then on their dossier a need to house the entropy in the ways I used to be attracted to myself among the things that are called-into-existence.

(39) Supplier of Those Words

It's a legitimate risk to read that remarkticle and not return its magazine back into the simple answer. Love be a baby to all the inhabitants of the city's quarters tonight. Remove that malignancy from the public library's reading desk... heresy from your bird's nest. And work into shape the flood so widespread it makes only the slightest impression ... a fleeting rebellion as we speak about our crocked specious (or is that special?) (i mean 'of the species') fate. An old-soundy voice that is found at the times for which the reader is the historical matter of contention ... says our generation can expect no love from the government ... because we've consumed it already by a method whose posture is indolence ... and now it's our fellow-person's work to cut us off. Moreover, all of us in preread vacuum ... no longer than first instance ... our exasperation, fluidly preposterous as it may be ... is flat conceit to quicken the application of death to life ... which, from the found perspective of the now old new deal is providentially merciful ... intention being obscure ... any longer than first instance ... need not be observed. Now let the minds who meted out those words too influentially and kind of stupidly ... or at least in a very limited heresy worked up by stupid adversarial impulse ... repeat the idea in the myth of that tower-building ... we breathing nitrous oxide like electrical spirit through our nostrils ... claiming anything to extend the same ... resound right into another question our vocabulary distance strives to impede. The dream of the infinitely small ... too so to observe ... but not hidden ... enjoined in phenomena. Every nisnomer ever dreaming on a tile ... unhidden ... singing rattle machinery to its sleep.

(40) The Works

Relentless assemblage of the question of the question to put the transcendence back into the science . . . of ordering . . . ummm . . . I'll have what is figured as the opposition . . . that is . . . I'll have precisely what this contemporary she . . . of my generation . . . is having. Is this wise? Interview with a zombie . . . the very same quoted . . . reassuring the format . . . our work is simply not amenable to top-down management. Interview with a reassurance . . . starts with a walk for the day . . . usually . . . otherwise there's the constant sense quoted as contained already inside itself.

(41) A Tone

Buy itself. Here stands this corrosion . . . painted all over with a leak to a monument something gives. The works . . . proved by the special names of their authors into public ownership . . . I begin to articulate the observation was the first to call smoke: time. Thus it's especially apt that the identical believes in you altogether . . . but prefers the jump over the little box . . . a middle classroomness irrevocably complete. He lets the air from the air that's listening to refute the Minimus . . . whose crudely sketched minimalism asserts two powers in any protracted monotheism or protecting dictatorship. Which caused some to explain the feeling of this place as threshers uprooted from an emperor-cult. A crypto-conscience turning the cherub into a leopard . . . fictitiously training fiction as the only means of production. How can I mitigate what I have to say about it so that anonymity is combined with earlier debts? Why . . . choose to see the bracket as silent and raise it through dialogue . . . for the fun of participating with ignorance . . . illustrating the relation between shapes as a parable for the fast-forward in parables. I know I owe you . . . the object I keep thinking I'm keeping . . . the ideas of thinkers who didn't make it by vows, prayers, punishments . . . anything to upset the theory. Why are you reminding me of the losers I lost sight of . . . the return of the two-way-link of earlier transgressions? Is the source of evil the thought of history as prompt . . . party gossip preparing a debt . . . an owing to the unsatisfactory show we will show later? Heaven here . . . like the store signs . . . points at right angles into hypothetical sentence of the street . . . American as importance . . . but not as far ahead as discerned or believed. Hustling these doctrines at the alien kennel . . . American pound . . . starving . . . it's impossible to impulse original attribution to the cause.

(42) Page of Big Mercy

Finds it hard to destroy what's been studied is stained by conduct sub-voice. Page through the operational half. Page we can consult for our investigation. We hung it out to witness . . . the need for a nice guy authority in interpretation . . . how formless could it be? So very rare so vaguely indescribable imitation of as much . . . you had it moved . . . to isolate a history to contain what can't be remembered . . . this is all that. Fails and is genre. Creating a cipherable incongruency of pace passed through the glean of the pool still fluctuating reflection . . . meant where I live my friends. Part of the source is discoverable as a left angle between writing the way description can't but evade suffering . . . the frame of experience always missing the person it abstracts from. These sources either do not occur at all or are some blazing coliseum of little holes . . . a method for memories as a compass does a solid to the degree a future positions past forms recurring. She blinks in the viewfinder . . . drinks to language makes it impossible to live . . . positioned in so many places you are not . . . yet can't be denied attachment . . . to what exists but can't refer to a place outside of reference . . . afraid of a description of its contents knowing it will evade the reappraisal of its fee. Afraid of the abrogation's unquotes will tickertape form to the urge . . . subjecting the description of its event to the dislocation of the subject they cause. . . . Enabler . . . drinks with some certainty . . . the material rise of very usual is shots to pieces.

(43) The Headlong Memorial

Because of the failure to remember . . . or for other reasons . . . we were identical fugitives in exposure . . . why a loved one is more painful and the witnessing more violent . . . all this presupposed in that unclear book or look . . . we gave each other . . . exact same theatrical cover to rid chance of a fitting removal. Yet the space of a few minutes is separated not only for its duplication . . . but for ownership for . . . consumed correlatives . . . a key is every bit as likely to be minute as a spire is. Like lower your eyes . . . a seamless scar to the back of the head . . . temporary name that continues to be transmitted . . . the connexion distance not to be found in this edition of the brain. So thank you for these additional rules . . . they can be walked as additional feet to the line . . . which though it was conveyed across centuries in this same world can only pretend that . . . guising through the echo lag of these quotes on quotes . . . poetic tone. Holy mouth of letters, Batperson . . . if I 'accidentally' wrote you a letter not called holy anymore . . . would it defile our thing?

(44) Wise Man Juniper

Why are you so . . . fill in the blank . . . then allow space for my response. The break was formerly indicated by its former . . . sea calendar misspelling. Or as then recommended . . . its former sea calendar misspelling formally indicated the break. Return not as way out as you think but as denial of way back in . . . the our sum machine some see as codified premise which actually presents the separation involved in turning it on. Dressing sexy in the popular mind . . . to move as entire body . . . to move slowly in that way . . . to grind sounds with an exactness . . . to be experienced by observers as seen . . . to feel as though everybody in the whole world is down on you. Dressing sexy . . . isn't vanity it's our assurance that both of us are not at distinctly the same risk.

(45) They Know Your Thoughts

I don't know how to receive your cross-accostation of a fact this remark wears. What's the arbiter doing when the cyst is dormant in the open hand . . . Answer: waiting to see if he knows your thoughts. I'm thinking on a page . . . the world's first wind-otter in the crosshatch . . . omitting arrangement for the master of the master of thought.

(46) The Hand Turned Colour Through Light

Because the latent image is engraved I try to send my hand forwards to the idea . . . but find only solubility. Performance is small unless speed is superimposed . . . as frantic time of exposure . . . would world the instance is illustrating. What describable purges we've gargled to! Seriously, what? This chap whose power is to command rabies by extending his hand to feed the beast chalk . . . what does he think . . . when the community's conception of power is a hopeless contradiction to the individual it appoints . . . exacting its presumably ordinary citizenship in an assail on history. Question: Do you know which of my sons does not see it? Answer: is the answer 'all of them' or 'each of them'? Surgically patterning a specimen of time that's most cutely old-world famine . . . so we can set the ambience with that healing old-world drought faith. And though this is the unambiguous order of replays performed . . . it's palpably useless . . . the whole of it . . . in establishing a real's mutual visitation . . . us regimented clientele report humbly through the pierced cloud as our community reannuls it.

(47) Surprisingly Every Time!

I was entertained by pantheism but we are the living dead . . . no, I was entertained by the labour of the pantheists we hired as interpretive acrobats to emphasize a religious system in which the human body could not be comparatively the figure of a goddess or god[dude/dard]. Anyone one can learn, surely (only), without delay . . . attention . . . yet our antecedent bread stop. A repertory, hallowed . . . this can't be denied . . . is inhabited entry ensnared . . . but is not directly chosen by our formative consciousness. Removing a great deal that we could have swung . . . this germ of the possible/impossible motive of performing towards ourselves. We do not know . . . simply a great deal . . . increase befitted only to a fear its form as circle . . . reservoirs because the city's a kind of linguistic full build we don't know. Whether my religious studies had the range of endeavour so as to derive such oath from a concept that it could rethread a new softer light in it . . . or not I ask . . . did I steel a facility, welded hyper-purification . . . when I undertook a devotion to all kinds of transgression? We just don't know whether our peops have soldered a doctrine of universal abode at every spot they are circled to have.

(48) Come On Fishy

Generation of separatists . . . playing thoughts on the shank bone . . . an illusion to shore their planes. Why can the choice points only be uncovered through the study of multiple texts? Why is the string still hanging from the arrangement . . . to isolate choice . . . the premise being that they removed the head rather than be struck by a boat flashed back past. A similar explanation can be given to walking in . . . his hand in the jelly . . . some sort of condensed lining . . . like too much is great in a mood of excess . . . who saw into the tram . . . purple. Feet as choice points you could distract by testing their conformity to the genre: 'the nature of walking'. Precious decades to cook this kind of language persisted . . . shown up radially from one writing moment to another . . . as though the shifts are curated by some mire sham up known as process. Take a piece of your control and conform it through an image analysis specific to the viewing angles common to print culture. Taste a Berliner. There . . . our own what . . . syntax . . . dated a sentience.

(49) Fist-e-Pure

Yes, it's true . . . I'm both at the seminar and not at all interested in the aphorism concerning molehill sizing and the social endorsement of my gripes. Do the dice see themselves mid-role like I vision the speakers' inner bearings as shadows of light that contract in performance? We have always called upon madpersons to deposit at night some disconnected knucklebones . . . to then be acrostically handset to expansion in the day-to-day by trustworthy first-rate scholars . . . lames its way into our drinking water. We're not the phrase-mongers Artemidorus so dislikes, no . . . we're attracted to the empirical, it's sexy . . . we're dedicated to our witness . . . we chastely judge to dislike each other. Likewise, miss or mister money body preps this, your narrow actuality . . . then your double-agent applies the violent force. Let's go a little further for our health . . . medical professional, capable of prescribing pot in our state, murmurs questionnaire . . . 'do you like suffering'? . . . adulterate silence . . . 'no' . . . 'do you like this little fawnskin purse'? . . . 'uhhhh . . . no' . . . You can't free yourself from your version of prison without another's help . . . give me your hand . . . and it knocks repeatedly on my head. . . . It knocks at the soft-hearted ones . . . it knocks at the usual sureties . . . it knocks many times . . . but there is no bank to go my bail. This unsuccessfully stupid read herring was read together as buckshot hind parts . . . a caption for inside us all . . . a counter based on transgressions.

(50) Awkward Entrance

In a legend we read the name of the store was released before we had pretended it was not encoded. Here . . . again . . . the tendency of finite power to tolerate plain and neutered synonyms alongside the supernaturally adorned ones. Though our purpose was surprise . . . we limited our symptoms to those tendencies already observed. If Jethro Tull says a word about our oath, tell him the image of a lip saying simulation. It's fully unable in an instant to actually torture him . . . just like his flute touching the general problem could neither bring about nor withhold the rain. Behave instead like in the legend . . . an unpleasantly happy wild-man.

(51) Epigraphic Piercings

Live in each other's parallels side-by-side without links. An inverse suite of the transposed graph . . . or graph switched with suite and suite with skin. That is, what seems to be happening to latter the term the more will be seen afterwards . . . posed in the majority of cases as having died within the crossing. All the more instant that its vicinity is doubled . . . out with litter of any contraption . . . the meaning of words sourcing the voices that say intrinsically ancient title . . . addicts all of them . . . investors of feeling. Just as it's . . . just as it's an investment response in my own sincerity to view irony and entitlement as aspiring and iniquitous authorities of indirect exposure. Broken bits is not the world . . . you know . . . but some localized citation of a probably later addition . . . what I call Emperors' rites . . . the rite of testifying that this is what's going on . . . the rite of hiding bad dreams (murderers!) in some slip-system of paratactical forgettings.

(52) The Plurality of the Worlds of Jacques

What kind interferences . . . homiletical sure . . . thing made to stop and to say to the profit . . . what have I done? . . . and how do I imagine it will get done? The agency follows the wait until they have asked you to . . . by whatever it means . . . getting it done . . . promote the long term by promoting the tonality of this dramatization. I am to promise some of my difficulties to the constraint for structural erasure. Done . . . omitted and re-present . . . she returns to find a manifesto in the balance . . . Jesus, the case is the same in the proof of others . . . thorough shorthand . . . yet still I had to be like lent for the dream to do the history more. Each shame metal . . . each evacuated bane . . . a tension is homage . . . to uncertainly rebel without in the healing . . . despondency in the kind medial interferences . . . distraught to dramatize completion as the best of for realistic pluralism.

(53) Face Rift

As though the wings of the covering were faces . . . as an order to avoid anthropomorphic projections. These wires that do reach . . . metaphor down . . . the morning hell hall in which all deities are alike. Same aura of all the equal faces of this mass avoidance . . . this moss that creates the wind's densed misunderstandings . . . is our accumulation of being without the sayings we are audience for. They are for mittens each . . . the roast of reusable error . . . same big deal to be broadcast . . . from the noise of the crowd . . . about this pool I can see from in back of the crib.

(54) The Harp of Failure

Do you know what I care about? Proof . . . Proof that . . . it is called failure because it turns back to look at us . . . with a world of difference . . . with a false mock stoic look like Epictetus says . . . if you don't get it (what you want) do suicide!! The mental vision of what is unthinkable . . . of an ungiven unreceived time necessitating invention and failure . . . because we live within a national organism repeating no discernable structural difference between nation and individual. So when a person apologizes in an apologetic country, she will be treated as the material of historical method within the theme of history . . . she must be forgetting to be prepared in advance for the need to abandon arising shapes. For your talent is to give an impression of the names of earth's orbital satellites . . . who transmit and receive from our inseparable harbour of only arrival . . . by punching like a rationally aggressive heart the eye of some ticket in hand . . . 'Papa', 'Goomi', (your parents), with their/its good and bad effects, allow you your protean faculty of adaptability. As in the thought of in between the counting . . . from the counting . . . the happening decline we attended in the rickety dogma shed was shaking in the formulating lung . . . altering the being against belief we violently associate our fall from . . . equivocal mould of graduation to the real world matrix of purposeful jobs.

(55) Silver Animus Employee

As an illustration there's the case of crowns . . . unfolded to display above the ears of your head a supplication. And yet there is nothing but beauty in the passing you emerged from void to . . . nothing but the incurable idolatory of your ears, eyes, nostrils, hands, legs, mouth in the vexation of their altering. I am extraordinarily in the smells of fried meat, accepting the sweet savour of personal sacrifice and humiliation . . . and it's at the same time the same darkened emphasizing room dissipates the certainty of reward by dispersing mirror of original form. My employer constructs a portable inner reward in the reply . . . inclined to lie just to lopsize the public pyre . . . I go no donkey was ever altered in the making of this Kong. Such an alien was excavated by the popular sense . . . the case of a few months ago replaced by a cleansing solvent . . . which is supposed to brandish a dead but amusing false room . . . but damn, when we placed ourselves in the exposure of that room we had a real money collection . . . and everything was back to the same price as before.

(56) The Manifold Worlds of Lives

A little ditty expressing attributes of eternity is so bound . . . to take a spacey place while the tune accompanies you in thought . . . the speaking napkin wiping upstream in is. Within the doctrine of omnimpotence each gape is all para-looking . . . genuinely smiles when it sees your pain . . . delighting in the reward you're collecting in some world to come . . . it's bring you your infinite child to opposite day. Unbridgeable contrast between on one side . . . smell sincerity accumulating on the other. Do you like how old your teacher is? . . . how old is your teacher? They know we know what we've done wrong . . . because they've evaluated our work forgivingly . . . because we were relentlessly impressive in the expression of our suffering and still we feel we got a lower grade than we really deserved. A list of synonyms for something not paradox not primitive not higher not absence not treatment . . . like a friend . . . calls out a friend as yourself for being them . . . any accusation in its improper place . . . trumps pronunciation. Continuing non-existence of antonyms necessary for present worlds . . . serrated appearance of . . .

(57) An Answer in Writhing . . .

In a series of calamities and in a great public distress we grew . . . more attracted to the easiness of an endless distress at the sign of completed attention. Mourning before its time in the meta fast days where we never knew we were eating . . . shaving . . . too close to be repeated we described a due diligence . . . and look at it now . . . damp again. Is this nude in or on jeopardy . . . symbolizing the gastro-intestinal rites . . . or writings? It's exhausting either, either way the validity of limitations recalls a coindicant by pointing to the words. That famous evil inclination who promised both there is no knowing and death by illumination . . . for the veil is the invention of the face . . . its scintillating thousands . . . aporetical synchosyllabic exposures of leaning into texts.

(58) The Neighbour This Name Indicated/Touched

Hello from the priestly disposition . . . its speech petrified of or maybe by the drug rep and gone. Entering into contraction with the passage of a greeting entering division with the words. A separate zoom through the pattern that caused this . . . grants you the terminal you-you may dwell in as well as the visual corpus you need to support it. With love and affection . . . the science of visualization played across your eyes beginning to be explained by access . . . aces (!) . . . according to the jump specific complexities. For Don Draper is neat, dexterous, apt, active, and suave . . . God be gracious to him and never grant him an inner-monologue voice-over again. Let's contradict a matter of fact . . . the widespread omission cannot be highly calculated enough . . . van the fan in mind hypes prospect . . . though it be naïve to do so . . . we've also given much thought to the sound-value of the gibbon's talk . . . which mind, it seems earlier than arbitrary. We give all this to me undefiled without mistake or corruption to the text . . . a lie free of moral impunity . . . except some residue everywhere of the sexual idea as the structure of God. It is a matter of fact . . . downright inappropriate . . . that the only influence of this fragmented voice-of-God is the unsustained regrettable everywhere . . . the tracing of repentance to be anything but constant . . . and by association named the thumbs in opposition to tap out and then into a genuine authorial vein.

(59) Mank the Transportability of Relation-ing

A defense allusion to inapplicability. They stood before their warded movement and said: 'Interesting are the forms of dislocation inasmuch as they can be doubled and tripled and doubled into exile'. We wonder what happened when, impelled by some annihilated parallel, we dismiss leaving because the nations of the world do not say 'the nations of the world'. The driven rules you see are loosely held in the speaker's masquerade of the system . . . it approaches some remarks like a bird moving from its nest is like a man wandering from his place . . . by inferring emphasis to the odds at promise in weather conditions as dialogic performance . . . an extraordinary coincidence . . . that is rather a similar but only curious coincidence to be found here as very old allegorical technique. A faithless committal to arrival which dwells on the teeth, myself, and bpN. A fifth of getting ahead is registering then alienating inheritance standing for right now . . . a third combines semi-relaxed instruction with the ashes of a not similar, no, a similar camp . . . and so fourth what's more similar . . . a humiliating gas incident or a homily quoted to someone who didn't exist (attributed to you)? The word by word action of begging your passage by hand is based on a question already asked: is it possible to owe speaking . . . to owe speaking to the story before the story begins? We have plenty of evidence to be aware of our disposal. To take and heed the proof of the structure belongs. Traces of artillery gloss behind the eyes . . . and will replace the pliancy of the hands. To redact the same ground editorially averse to the person who types method as explanation. Other names either . . . placed . . . classified . . . materialized . . . for I am objected to a joke . . . maturely any identification with measuring . . . and consequently the exhibit time of any discovery matter.

(60) The Worker B

Alien to the spirit, most distracting is the . . . what did you say? . . . table monadic again in our postmortem age . . . wherever you go you make a table into a person there and then a person out of the sound. The weirdo maker I am is a personification of the sound as a person on the table of 'word' and 'void'. We should be a whole chapter on the name 'boy' in this country (and I won't even not mention the racial violence in this) . . . as if they began their address to us the good and upright male worker: 'Boy . . .' . . . and oh boy since they're too fucking big on to be spoken to . . . we go into a lengthy and rambling explanation to be blamed for. Is the remedial really to be taught? What about the further remedial? The thing in which this word tendency can be increased to show . . . is between parallelism as truth and prescriptive chronicling amidst a crowd of describing it . . . and in our explanation there is more rather . . . to go outside a distance . . . of its big written insufficient. Yet we still have our work as our disposal . . .

(61) World of Rex

Frequently tied (up to three hundred times) in leather ties around the cornea this typo is rare enough. The name of D.'s dog carved into the gun rack with a quarter cheated this chance of connexion. Sometimes . . . without substitution or spillage . . . there is no fulfillment in returning to childhood. The cerated tuckamony of bedtime goes repealed by a knot in the rope. Waving technique . . . Very.

(62) Straight Show Now Tell Me

They meant to say that our suffering is always less than what we really deserve. Chugs an exposed video gapped in the kind of things they say. Dome has unconscious movie with God . . . as captain anger or . . . captain righteous. He pounds the last slider to prove there is no immovable limit. An age of spit from my anonymous interlocutor the . . . hire the doorway . . . two people being added to this thought to all parties . . . through it, X got stoned to die . . . shaped her generation as a domed garment . . . sceptered it by asking . . . would you rather be exalted or crucified (like Morrissey before her). Especially domed alone for a second fast . . . rating towards them. Truce-hammocks excessively lined to order a watershed moment rated . . . for team baby butt . . . was swearing . . . she loved her.

(63) Like

This term is older than any what any perspective might bring to us period. It's used to emphasize that Mosaic Indices and/or Indecisiveness did not actually enjoy the game of slow directorial loss . . . but grinding it first in the mouth of contemporary hailstorm . . . what does that get us beyond? Aesthetically writing, the well-played riddance of repeating reference corrupts the performance of you . . . so it's difficult to doctor faces once reconciled with the-ones-who-love-them. Now the graved escape an errand reserved even by their limits for a question . . . my insecurities on par infinitely with friendship into the hood of a hoodie. Wonder why the heretic is considered a phony? The whole world order hammered down conditionally . . . connexion alarm moving in accented dark along passages copied by older works . . . Surprise!! Doubt cigarettes legible to crayon . . . illegible to oneself.

(64) Hoodie Up/Hoodie Down

Like specifically a model . . . owed to take the place of the earlier the place . . . all the forces hinting that some all-important victual is monologuegically trapped in self-possession. The idea hollowed from the company to the fact of the advertisement in question was a veneration for the belonging through love of motherhood . . . 'my' or 'mine' own mother or motherhood. It's the fabric that makes sure that standard distinctions between internal and external occurrences remain later transcendable. It's the packet as leather handshake between two same-sized texts . . . holiness and sanctimoniousness. Which sampled from the epigraphical . . . and which from the apocryphal? One was liberally severed . . . the other evenly. This was to be fully dealt with in school . . . but a pubescence brought to these forces only ledged them into an array of overheralded thirds . . . the possible threats a parked car might be felt to not feel in its very isolation . . . but very often . . . to make some you . . . some severance past sung forwards . . . by the feeling above of its sub-singing . . . what facts we had not shown not done.

(65) If I Here

Even before we are born our thoughts are like flying wax cylinders . . . soaring stored and storing within the spun garments of collective memory. See this as typing . . . the steps I will grind in my sleep future . . . as if someone were drawing up from a drawing a drawing on a drawing. It's a carrying of impact into exclamation . . . foreseeing water in the gap . . . between the hawk you hold in the dream and those situation receiver towers. Both were preceded by a growth again in the place of their going . . . down with the shit of personal desire.

(66) Consumerist

Teaches that sandals without a discernible brand name are automatically fired out of use after thirteen steps by the consumer away from the consigned service area of the merchant. Four months I was lard in the service oven . . . bargaining in anonymity . . . with the double meaning . . . Creator and Maker. This reminds me of the model they hired . . . she would never allow a quotation to question her . . . quiet description of canvas . . . and then the photograph . . . comes across like instances . . . back to the chiropractor . . . emphasis on the latent image . . . possibly some end things. Instance the latinate names floating there . . . the poet Max Bill . . . for Maximum Billing . . . on this receipt makes a word worth quitting . . . coming across sentences in the reign's trans-possessor.

(67) The Portation of Thought

Inverted record to place . . . similily . . . neglect on the exposed heat this name as interference. The flame itself disturbs to thought a hopeless contradiction blended into the labour of knowledge . . . the chief trick in the poof of annulment. But we need a community to deliver our thoughts to the helm of a corresponding adulation . . . and as notes are spaced in our thought . . . we indulge in sieging guesswork with seriousness . . . militant exhaustion that forged that regrettable beastly bullet, the dictionary. Listen, my girlfriend is coming over, bedecked by the scruff of neurosis to author together each of our forgivenesses. These last few years . . . talking by trial and error . . . we've learned to let contradictory requests send unfulfilled. We've learned to let the horrible initial emotion get paid by the parochial bosom of commercialism we're in. Lost credit card retroactively forgiven . . . letting opposites a bi-convex history light-writing.

(68) Truth (for Corporations and Cooperatives)

One cannot fail to express uncertainty in amazement . . . since we have to begin with an edifice, rather than dissolved, everywhere a chorus of tentative tiles . . . cracked in place by the renovation polemics of Viagara and the like . . . convincing us the constant creative outburst of our emblems' power is dogmatically avoidance of pity . . . and not *vice versa* . . . where it ascribes the omni-radius of deep thought so profoundly and avowedly . . . as to entitle an anticipation of immeasurability around any word or similar problem. This is why the lost parts . . . without being aware of it . . . imparts . . . a spiritual sense that seems typical . . . for us an almost doctrinal impulse . . . but is nevertheless genuinely moving . . . redemptive as the symbol passes almost sacredly but without preaching . . . between smaller and larger mirrors as they emerge this morning . . . descending out from the walk-up . . . and celebrates the bright passage of its inner dissolution. This analysis is more than likely . . . a reply to a certain interlocutor of mine . . . a human being . . . who in one of our frequent discussions . . . illegitimately forbade me to change size . . . and then this cropped up . . . that art's truths . . . its allegorical insights . . . like Noah's ark . . . only find their coinage so to speak in the messenger . . . the messenger's proud trouble with co-habiting . . . message writ large on a large wall that itself spells 'painful slogan' to the whole earth as boasting messenger . . . directing its slow rotating low bow to the greater universe it contains. No wonder this (and its opposite) gave rise to subsequent perfunctory dismissals of those claiming underlying sexist and racist prejudice . . . it quite markedly leaves no room for even the smallest penises to be shown in walking . . . and is nothing but the attempt to exploit a foreground of authenticity . . . on account of the looking-glass-like conditions of conversation which pattern a system of signs as indispensible . . . however remote a distance they may be placed in . . . and demand touch at every distinction.

(69) A Consolation Icon for Every Sign

This is styled the house of nostalgia blessed by its mourning. Yet pained by sadness's denial . . . preferred desire . . . turned fetish to usurp its place. Make up your mind . . . concerning this . . . every fifteen years, secular illness stands you up to rend from you your supplicatory prayers. This is standing designed to supplant the drunk cup who looks at me like that's not true. We speak through the ear we shall drink it through . . . the former ear. You look at me like that's . . . a plan to comfort the mourners through a lien on ego.

(70) The Righteous Tune to Tetris

The sermon we begin with a sermon chilled in time beforehand speaking grievous things with contemptuous pride. The luck of the circumference before him . . . so devours spaces without knowing why. Restake that argument. Rephrase those step echoes. Does each body behave like an unavoidable metaphor, 'deaf and dumn' to the translation it's being tied to? In the name of forgiveness please explain how any two attributes could be combined . . . could lapse into anything but the eyes of their connexion . . . some sort of omniscience curdling in the mock moments we know and see as hosts to our hearts and sinews. Only a few. Only a few even in their anger . . . the sacrifices . . . strayed from making an origin and concerned themselves with the exaltations of static metallic points removed from the souls of the cattle they ingested . . . only a few fully identify with the argument they are . . . advances. Looking for manhood you (he or she) in all the strength games had not dreamt what she (he or she) had done and remained willed by showing that you . . . are not quote a spiritual person . . . to accept only seen reference but believing in your plural . . . future. He (she or he) tries to make a muscle . . . it toggles between the event of isolation and that of rearrangement.

(71) Earnings on High Risk High Yield Ventures

Pseudepigraphic bit in the mouth . . . replenishing psalms in the tone archive. A little respect for our heroes of dust . . . please . . . goes a long way for the investment . . . finite but not even close to countable. If a woman should dream she is feeding her vagina crumbs of bread and cheese as though it were a small animal . . . let's just leave it at that . . . reversing a gender bias. The leaving is capable of shining . . . the shining capable of leaving. Yet not still, not moving, there is still the bribe of event . . . and our frames' artificial identicality is qualified as only their artifice. As one of the oldest in a family of twelve, I've been enumerated into the onus of responsibility . . . it's my job to know this use in our period as the change shit way past safe was already in archaic times . . . bound by the security of a future ex-change. I mean I'm getting like a hard-core emulsion complex . . . like I gotta get out from this house. Fumigating on the back porch now . . . my alibi in the tobacco . . . revelation in the tobacco . . . turning degrees of relevance production to instance saying/hearing float.

(72) Whine Quality Analysis

This, which remains our first, asks does the quality, that is the labour conditions of the inherited method, affect the reciprocal potential in the subject's artifice. If yes, I'm really curious to see if we'll figure it as stretching fluidly above people into another moment . . . or perhaps rather as sub-verb gulfing constantly . . . across that quick part between insult and inquiry. Regardless, it's that crossbeam that knows no limits . . . it's how far we'll follow a speculative unicorn to see a radial curvature in the sun's corpus . . . and then in the false overture of our verminally disastrous character . . . fail to sustain the particularities of this witness. Keeping the spread fresh on a ready table extended to all. Ostensibly open to the next order . . . scattered . . . by the power-leak of this dispersal.

(73) Infinitesimal Wealths

We determine our response to each entreaty by the lend in the recognition of self-hood . . . its nurturing of a sensual ground of incoherent transfers . . . the community bend in community's metaphor. And in our supplications we must remind ourselves that attention can be paid . . . instead of given . . . can, in its pointing outways . . . record a harsh treatment rerouted as expected necessity . . . determining which excesses are understandable. As counter-present instances we are invited to understand this. Do not continue on the lone small reply . . . on the homilies like this you owe to displace will by concluding . . . nor as string of isolation to the premise of uncovering in the hands some trauma of the feet . . . encountering this resonant gap as stolen chat of eternity to eternity. We can't suspend our tonal function, right . . . so not the new nation again . . . or this f-ed up old condemn yourself . . . goddamn us. I'm roughly trying by degrees some richness we overpaid for . . . based on a truth story lining up the speakaphone[a-thon] to the choicest padding for this empty story . . . try to flick into an acoustic multi-angle by chance yes.

(74) Hymn Without Effort

The puzzling sign expands faith, expands a history devoted to impulse. Look at not at . . . a mention . . . derives experience from the imagination of its telling. Term falls firm in the repetition in your brakes. It was rarely a house that stood the test of signs . . . I walked away doubtful . . . walked back again . . . walked back away again, always looking doubtful . . . always looking up. Whether what happened next was a variety of silence . . . a system, a communality, appeared only in its fragments . . . what was known was it was . . . difficult to explain. Pitch heightens as well to the stumbling-block . . . we draw . . . slowing things down from. As to the activity it is . . . steeped in the parallel injury. Barrenness, show me where it's arranged again and I will move us again to the city revealed. Can you remember when I shut up . . . the future walking edge . . . for your judgement echoes . . . a protective vest through the siphon . . . then mom and dad what. Take away the considerable patience and witness . . . the machine corroding the imagination of its flesh. Like if the kid goes 'I looked but I couldn't find it' . . . don't believe them . . . and if they're like 'I didn't look but I found it', yeah also don't believe them. And don't buy into those theological machines repeating 'seek and ye will find' . . . I mean they're right . . . but finding it doesn't solve any big problems . . . we search for fainter darker problems. Whatever happened . . . to the rejection of final answers . . . it's not some final answer. Whatever . . . produce quality turning independent . . . films some dream of dough . . . some dream of bread.

(75) Big Mane

Are we to remember the day when the day is reconstructed by ear, throat, and nose air . . . big bend along its torso to look for presence behind the real thing. The handbook they speak of so elderly. One to the right . . . one to the left . . . this makes sense because we're feeling guilty . . . like guilt can change but innocence can't. Well, reason doesn't solve our problem . . . except to necessitate delay . . . without which meat would be exclusively substituted for intention. Because the transcriptive text alone in some as the archive of reason must submit itself to another orderability that is even more unrealizable and can't assure any service of any service that would either dissolve or meet intention. Instead of guilt why don't I fill a space with the attempt to divine aptitude . . . here here . . . on a placard read up . . . on what you got.

(76) In the Service Industry: We Who Spoke

They feel as a native you already own the crime . . . you need to . . . for the dispossessive blankness they were gifted and deserve . . . crime is their destroyed origin . . . known to them bruised only by the blame who used it. They feel a 'most people' are under the discussion . . . is this ok to bring this into discussion . . . we simply spoke and the world replied: 'there are uncommunicated constructions it's not possible to understand', Is this one of the characteristic roles of our art . . . now on a categorization tour stretched from the time of writing to the time of language . . . shifting so to speak . . . multiple shrimp along the same preventative skewer of the same word? Some of the ancientest approaches known to us by name discovered this predetermined risk in an old Sumerian charm . . . words proportionate parts melancholy and mirth . . . and used in antiquity . . . as a compass. Owing this discovery to how or why people empty the spacialized body of thought . . . we trace this surface to some infernally reflective stage where iconic 'The Shepherd Gone King' stands rapping the dissociative factor into some mixed response to insuperable space around 'hymn'. Mixed with emptiness assets, the grid is then delivered, revolution to them the me out of all . . . I'm inclined not to agree of course . . . something not presence.

(77) Variance in Spectacles

Or subtitle: An owing to the unseemly number and character of errant texts. First order . . . to suspend an off-putting conjecture . . . defer immediately . . . wipe on grease to not read the words . . . neither the business matters nor the daily diary of our ancient annoying behaviours. As the language and context prove . . . all reading is addressed to this age . . . all spongy inside. Yes the words speak of words as already human, but this occurs once in the proclamation of its also . . . identical with what you might need to do . . . before to be well-known . . . that is . . . stick the erase board the words were written for on the absent acne-to-be in the oil. Losers to some nth degree . . . and this time you wanted to hear it . . . these days a pressure apparently . . . the way they speak to the words . . . starch know-it-alls . . . them proselytizing fathers of yore. Like what we see can be observed as change . . . therefore change is necessary. Sound. Imitation . . . inevitably to judge itself . . . thus also has a corny divine purpose in life . . . to bring us nearer to each other . . . until a huge electro-magnetic pulse removes us into simultaneity from our surroundings.

(78) A Mouldy Ology of the Monad

The parasite of deserving anything... let alone a new theory of language that beams stretching below the street... level with me now... for the hundred thousandth noxious divination. In a check rhythm science here is a grammar symbolics of poetic connexions which are evented and transformed like any public sphere: (1) the ruthless hock in speech; (2) acidity; (3) locality; (4) joining mythology (*e.g. Shira Princess of Power*); (5) opiates; (6) luck bill; (7) the brogue of anticipation; (8) second sight or alternately anything raab (*e.g. broccoli or spinach raab*); (9) second sight or alternately lettuce in no. 2; (10) second sex or a series of two archways; (11) our cancelled menu; (12) stick it to the ok; (13) modest mayhem (*alt. reading: hidden ox genitals*); (14) wind shove (hiccup); (15) wind sock (hike); (16) wind smack (reliable); (17) histamine on the break of wind; (18) the winded messiah aches; (19) wind capsizing wind in a hole (*alt. readings: wind caps off the wind; wind capsules off in the wind*); (20) first prize goes to 'the wind-win situation' by Ezekiel Ruth-Acker of Hector, KS; (21) a clutch of nasty wind cakes; (22) the recognition of fuck-ups (and the racket not to change them); and (23) net or [and/or] gross temperature. To show this... is just doing my work... not a revolt more like... burned 'I Put an Oath on You' acts to give the lame substitutive condition of theorizing our youthful virilities... 'I Put an Oath on You' just some government hard-on that its work of era aura was really accomplished... but cannot be enumerated in this place... the traces we find change revved up in their casing to not be revealed before us. Are these vacant boxes then... shifting a special attention to border layers... just the old low deed? Between the show and the under-ace . . . between the difficulty and the scab and the difficulty of the scab . . . an uncoded participative production is imagined . . . and a really lengthy encouraging dialogue which . . . though it can't be enumerated here . . . shows clearly that such a use is available at our age.

(79) Privileging the Primer for Revolt

His old man scripting the needs of the class . . . insigning the skeletal document the group was responsible for digitizing. The same was not unknown to the speculative and annoying flicks made at the ear of the godhead. Mine to write to chips all about the projection screen. So to look out of the hypocrite shoe at the large expanse of interdependency . . . rhymes with indeterminacy . . . whether it is mourning or still you who recognizes the condition of seeing for the weeks it is . . . perfection as an obvious question to the tucked-in smallness of that mass hypnosis of non-specific event. So that's why there are instances where owner is the older conception . . . of the circuitry of what you know delivered its ignorance necessarily to the importance of meaning. Some things to remember . . . are hot to marry in this vertical disposal . . . comparatively . . . the case who does this . . . seeing as what you know . . . is the loss you make to mean . . . you are one for the phase. Suddenly in the bilingual look . . . without benefits 'cause of its inside verbs . . . not just the online womb . . . but the online camera and all exposed to a contrivance of utopian globalism . . . zapped as in the old futures' seeing to our cognitive know-how . . . by renewing our address we voted daily.

(80) Shock Until Now

I am asking for summary but you say this only occurs once . . . this instantiation of this form given here for completeness's sake. Our intention then is to enumerate this recovery in a quick yet gentle-eyed fashion . . . we are looking to land aware of these feet . . . but to suggest we are not following explanation . . . tonally. Jealous of this silence. Platforms you see are standardized . . . just like there's no outside to the thornbush for whatever makes the thornbush consume itself and speak. Possible trade: a schedule of both failed and successful attempts to understand the text around me . . . for it wasn't long ago the crystal text was on the desk being and modeling geological. Impossible trade: I'm thinking of freaking out complaint . . . for it might be unethical . . . this delight in any nodal intervention. 'What kind of memo did your impermanence get'? . . . 'Do you mean to suggest I'm not aware of this . . . process'? Rest assured I will personally track this down this.

(81) Pattern Prodigy Conversion

He desired to make partner . . . duped by who understands preempting the end of the story. Owed to account for the work that he did . . . the names and numbers . . . names and numbers . . . the sufferer is the person who tries to manifest the material of suffering and suffers in this failure . . . as any formal constraint receives its processing code from the index of names . . . yet caves in transgression, still disputing its translation of blindness, to advance infirmity's dominion. Alarm bells a vine around the clumsiness of claiming innocence. Its tolerance for approaching sexuality by detailing conventions of the intensity frontier. And how much sabotage and pain descending on the 'potent' needs of a man is instrumental to subjecting women to a violent cloud of unshakably ridiculous masculine power. Alms . . . alms . . . alms for combining this in my mind with my propensity to put trust in all but oneself. Lewis Bayly, Bishop of Bangor, anonymous anonymous author of The Practice of Piety prophesighed . . . sheesh . . . in the future a burn by friction yet felt to be added, that which may turn the wish of each individual so acknowledgeably to that of an other that various true views should amount to no right thing, and no wind, so to speak, should be even potentially fulfilled, &c. The history of the metaphysics of figuring interpersonal space (known otherwise as ethics) ought to appear quite differently than that picture to those who know it. Again, the cruel fucking adage expressing that such and such is already known to and presumably uttered by many people got sand in it. Can't the panic just occur as central operating tissue, tolerant as any good solution to counter-punching difference?

(82) Carob Berekhas

Anti-image invoking what beauty is . . . as if merely by being dead we might find the hymnology apparently looked for. Seeking appearance of disbelief for specific instances . . . everlasting favorite on the look of the door before her . . . the research from the end of the beautiful stretching *s* letter of miles to orphan the willing. The most cynical thing the ghosts ever said was their motions of what it was to be apparent . . . above all creatures. And in these creaturely thoughts I invoke the rose whose experience is both yardly and beautiful . . . imported you know from crates of wind . . . through the gap in the crisscrossed slats of the wooden fence . . . where the thrash of accumulation tubs the abstraction between one thing and another.

(83) Stuck in Addition

Hopes for an arithmetical sum painted sidewisely in our euphoric vein. Interior lectern, part dolorous, for nothing escapes its fee. Double the automatic simultaneous pariah hunkering to relinquish the viral squid from its own duplicate . . . sensorium, ill verging on abducted by its martini's momentum. Heaven, I'm in heaven . . . when I went bald I gave my beautiful hair to heaven . . . and though I'm no believer in a transcendental God . . . I sensed direct from up on high . . . that my well was literally overflowing with vows of such unedited remove . . . that chance would have at it . . . to provide a fresh, running alert of the joined emergence of cultic and legal forces in language. This is the latest strength to be mocked into not disappearing . . . in that vanity vanity lament. A beer for every caller this evening calling from a bar . . . you got the angle . . . you're a keeper . . . and you can't keep a keeper, can you?

(84) Bitter Brand

The rumor of a day today speaking which arcs a cubicle bound for the sky . . . the tired eyes around our skin appearing us to find that portrait of nowheresville . . . some trust fun reply to the pointing in the surround of this room an audience observed. Dave is then introduced to the people . . . Sara is introduced to the people . . . words to that effect introduced to the people . . . then introduced . . . Rhino . . . Anacreon . . . and the Golden Gate Bib (Splinter and Shredder standing hand-in-hand by the neck-hole). Thus, by removing only a single shape we got clobbered by the musak . . . muzak faster than facial response to warp the countenance of the corresponding shapes. Ring a word use in the future world pattern yielding in the speaker's sense of accretion. Others at the generic tint logging the outer roll call we find . . . easing a list backwards into the bigger-kids' pool.

(85) Reincarnation of Agreement

In spite for best intentions . . . need was fought through eye of identity . . . risk submission of article to the magazine apt mistake . . . was your lost son recognizable to the forms entrusted to him. Matchbox car hanging like a jewel from the neck of a mule . . . and you owned my ass for that jewel. Ours of first rate melancholy see . . . then theorize the record the turn of its award. What the basis promises an audacious twist . . . however that form abandoned car be relied upon . . . it may have pitted stops and spindles resisting monadic tune of the place-same. Never try to make one thing . . . the idea in this that there is no arbitrariness unsubmitted to the magazine fate of juxtaposition as the augur of this fate . . . and name another double that problem . . . classical style painting entitled Madonna and baby Rav Yosi ben Halafta. Meanwhile . . . she was out doing a whole basket of figs . . . that is inscribing the good Socratic dialogues on figs and handing them to beggars. God, that's cake! That's cake meaning . . . I forget . . . manifesting unknowable exterior.

(86) Friend?

The after-effects were divided, teacher taught, into three different parts, each of two evictions. These six are called friends . . . motors tied to an open account in time . . . to dispel a fever inside a word on . . . the back that's kind of rationally behind your back. These six are called friends . . . and overwork to spread among the blurring of targets . . . away we can avoid error . . . though an actual extra falls in the human and animal films alike . . . hit skeet of some proviso . . . stilling a certained force of the copses' decal arch about the teeth of our friends' faces. Smile friends without trouble . . . for all time not lost is shared . . . not yet getting ready for what will be bestowed upon them . . . if all doors stand open to combat . . . doubt of this . . . kind, earnest grapple with a paving breeze. A shitty old punishment we should've neglected, but could not resist our opinions on the subject . . . our loose spittle heading out sideways . . . reigning back in as fetters on our suffering.

(87) By-Knock-You-Lars

The clash for students who think 'abstract' as 'it can't be thought'. The latest in last period acting who cares before submitting once again to the wrong bratwurst . . . its redaction through the mini-hog-cartel of assigned body. This all links to the power of scheduling or power-scheduling . . . since . . . as they're wont to say . . . the one who points it out was probably the first to apply it. I need to establish shows we like right away in common when prompting into reliability this pedagogical ethos of encouragement. Like bird-watching as a refreshing introduction . . . as a class we install video cameras close to the nests of rare birds . . . create a bulletin on which we'll note contemporary developments . . . then use the variants in our reportage to open ripe dialogue about our development and flexibility as writers. First class, right . . . my sweet sweet righteous bastards . . . rethinking welfare through the deafening stone of a hangover hollowed in the automated bell's twenty seconds of distilled order . . . we've each just begun to find the revamped brioche-in-hand older and soothing . . . worth one in the imagination. Not that this is enough for either the label or sustenance . . . all concepts proselytize the prose purely according to need . . . needing to bury the idea in the ass of an opponent's wing every half ours it leaves. Speaking of the end of white noise in point and reference . . . here is the shown part part shown . . . we signaled time to each other, signed if we can rely on anything in experience and . . . if this isn't the summoned try to affect us . . . and should we be summoned to bite our brethren . . . I mean we were going places put together sitting down. I mean I trust in a together us people . . . to frequently enjoy our food *and* our food muzzle, haze ourselves together, pig out our eyes, destroy the popularity of any name to vindicate our own . . . coming back at them with the difference we husk . . . exceeding sentience in spite and slash of loss. Look, it's by no means impossible that these speculations project a dollar bill noticeably spun out over Lake Superior . . . an atmospheric marriage of finance and wind, like 'kid, don't go in for that' . . . to be beamed up and rather indiscreetly prodded and analyzed by some too unloving language . . . with that motion saucer suspended there . . . believing the still presence of it meaning . . . to stand at the point of its dwelling-place . . . restructuring its value through the wind o'er the lake. This is not anymore about anyone one being entirely . . . other people . . . but the leaps in juxtaposition being amenable to unsettling our participation . . . why they won't be easy to drain people down the light they throw like a straight visor flicked by this enormous holograph. Finally . . . using hiccups to join in the problems of today . . . what I can hope to get out of . . . TV ascribed to me unfurling in the reference of these instants. Again if this me is pixelated it's only because it was meant to be smaller . . . it isn't even the most noteworthy binary container seen here.

(88) Hyper-Rapport

A sketch that used to go on forever . . . the nocturnal dialogue between a human and their horse. They say to the horse, night-capped skull resting on the dividing bale: 'Formerly . . . I mean yesterday . . . I led thee to water . . . the pendulum which bonds between us tensed a succeeding pendulum to air the leftovers of an extroverting structure . . . and consequently . . . you did not drink'. In scale I've roamed the whole system but still I've never seen what I've seen in the sea. The soft key to explaining coherence . . . endemic to the full page . . . foil screens disrobe the group into an app to background an option of when we are and or are not met. The latter replies: 'The problem sets up a crisis for me . . . the problem is this instance . . . nay, any instance . . . is a rheumatic environ of cultural dependence for me . . . on you . . . my strategy for moving is your strengths and weaknesses . . . your cadences, not my digestion and feces, say . . . say I proposed to myself . . . when looking on high into the reflective surface of water . . . that thou was about to drown me . . . kissing me into the larynx of that liquid oven'? Does the waste of ammo justify the same . . . to lob the glassware out over the gauze wall to watch its break now syncing? And has the bassist's doo so tired of duping age by going 'sick 'em' to the id? Or don't alight with balking . . . at what is amiable to the giant . . . what is amiable to the giant OMG upon heights? It is the OED anally entiring your space to privatize the word bomb. Invasion whatever . . . note-taking to rope it . . . put immunity in a position where it might fail . . . and then we have a script!

(89) Oh Heathens and Heavens

I incline to see into this name more forcefully than I can settle on any one spot . . . while our prototypes are dispersed then superimposed into lasers of only interior meaning and function. Very veil of the rough . . . assuming of a cryptographic aspect to the name . . . difficult to lift definitives out of. One thing is not certain and that is that the name is only use . . . that is, the reservation of a put in time. No difference here between ritual and law . . . into the poem . . . that which above all acquires some kind of faith for its readers. Here was the best of toasted ravioli and we couldn't taste them, &c. It really takes so little to get us full while we wait for so much . . . for from under our wait is ourself figured above it . . . the waist of experience, the reduction its unpassed-into futuring. You hyped it so I did too . . . or were we just working together to corroborate the sanctified role of temptation in our lives . . . that we try not to repeat itself, yet that's what all we do. What we probably meant was that from under the repeating is ourself figured above it . . . too familiar to have objected to any name . . . just belonging to the lateraled futuring of such an older or shorter place.

(90) Money Wrap

Although the motto was supposed . . . its value's in the name . . . juxtapproved by the congress in the name . . . likewise coined as a reminder . . . of oneself . . . some sexy bangled bummer in unison . . . a come-uppance for all the maxims pledged. It is not impossible to assume this wad . . . the anthem for our Pilates spread to some greyer abroad . . . establishing a religion every time it's challenged. A quick tally front for some unknown. Introduced to importance by the cut of its acceptance . . . the cored peg is used as an escape push . . . it immolates punctuality but only musically . . . and only for those it chooses. Like the image of 4 out of 10 returning . . . hair whittled down to violent crews . . . wealth and property to soothe a distant hate. Prisoners these last four years of drought . . . the mutilation of salad to a stale prism of shrunken veg . . . we mention finally . . . getting to the point . . . if you're still in some jail . . . now this doesn't have to be an actual steel-bars jail . . . what's important here is that your imprisoning institution is adamant that you're in there because of your own actions . . . and so your work is contrition . . . we mention finally . . . getting to the point . . . if you're still in some jail . . . some adamant repetition you're here because . . . of your own actions . . . your work is contrition . . . eternally . . . for someone else.

(91) A Peaceable Move

Trying to figure out the slaloms from a door within . . . as what's worth doing smack in the middle of the day . . . versus our girlfriend and boyfriend at night. Now let's say we're thinking about what we almost saw . . . piecemeal . . . police work . . . a pillar of smelt in the sea of estimated recording time . . . though we are faking to reconcile this conflict. So exit subject interrupts us in the midst of our peace meal like any plural side to explain something in the print up . . . in the print up holding those back that up summoned away from within the door within . . . some TV show spun off of the movie. Nice screen capture. You can definitely trace two things at any one time which is exactly what I was thinking. Feels like the drones are protecting us from exactly what we have to collage . . . noticing away that we steal from these guys. So keep our bricks nice . . . two books for two bucks . . . as between it goes around its efforts come to spin. Like a house made of books to promote the sale . . . or just a Target gift certificate. That's what I wanted to say . . . so what . . . this represents a way to attack it . . . probably rolling the two dice fives with five different release points . . . but ultimately trading back straight up your origami book for my tadpole . . . the one I like to call Who's Who in American Football 1986.

THE NAME

I.

Pronunciation

The future's constant apology was concurred inna photo . . . in wanting this past very idea of namelessness. Thought has only names . . . is a reading of Ted Berrigan's . . . trying to mess shit up . . . for all futures that come without us. Maximus-a-million of the next ailment . . . already altered towards growth in guesses . . . to reconcile our grip off with the doctrine of our adopted nation. A middle name of ancestral reminders torqueing emphasis out the till again and again . . . we is free for the dogma of our age.

Forgetting the attitude I'm trying to tarp between us . . . to have undone to have felt as current . . . apparently, I couldn't divert our attention so long as to widen our longing into oblivion. Who knows . . . to boot . . . the influence they see gone . . . as influenced pronounced gone . . . as un-circular . . . collapsed cursing into supreme message. Because the public clams . . . down in the deepest reverence . . . whenever dared to . . . extend discrimination into some electoral technique . . . some policed designation . . . naming the beyond quantity of differents . . . public . . . threat to personall . . . very sickness . . . we repeat . . . I am sick of . . . complaint as compliance . . . but when we began to speak out against the right moment . . . the ms. was revised . . . just before . . . to if one dare mention the Name in anti-alien ordinary time they are guilty of death by total irony . . . for then we can't even speak of blaspheming the Name without a tonal hint of blaspheming it that shits all creatures to its rhythm.

And to ask . . . was he the one a-sassin that we dreamt of between 4th and Constitution . . . the one whose power/hallucination was . . . transmitted in a lot of sighs . . . the inability to adequately express. The body decaying in a lot of sighs in the question of its new material. Gained from the duration of the liquid capsule where the important release is delayed . . . an inner space in decay . . . visible through the old reading matted that anyone could possess sympathy . . . that experience as information is death.

There is no doubt there was at once a time a time a time when this prohibition was entirely halled in where what iterates was more or less any kind impossibility low in to barb the Lame. Divide it into many recent mistakes not to mention . . . the extraneous report . . . to date the writer in their exaggerated dedication . . . to you the real to real transmission of language . . . illegible scrawl. To begin or end is just always a coding of that . . . if you're waiting on the ancient . . . I see no way around this . . . dating the hypostasizing time . . . attempt too to communicate some lowest common . . . democratic end to the Names.

To say there was no law, just ordinary conversations and greetings . . . you're in the genetic orb . . . partly observed, part immunity . . . prohibited into existence. Adopts not kidding in view of asking . . . what is a generative act in eternal return loop . . . eternal forgiveness having lobbied foreign entities for our rhythm's end. Yet having altogether seen only frequency, the view stopped short must have risen especially violently to scope the tarp . . . to rope the dictionary back to a positively or negatively charged papyrus . . . to sexualize the editing code of some textual past as a dangerous amnesia . . . so liable to be violated.

Yet instead of the gone wild trying not to break the Geiger counter . . . a historical lasting . . . no more than a salt has your topping . . . turns back to pull your paralysis and gives you a pal . . . pronunciation like some frozen hide. We won't know the reason for this special reform . . . balance literally cuts up historical decline into contemporary worth . . . its substitute some camp tradition . . . all boys gone to all boys bunk . . . like are you waking yet buddy? Headphones turned low enough to hear the information outside. Through the thought limits of perfect eyesight . . . cussed bigger than this attention . . . the next to you person . . . the custom of what I wish I didn't know substitute . . . crusted off from my . . . elec . . . tron . . . ic voice . . . who pivoted our galaxy's mortality towards my mum and said . . . electronically . . . do . . . you . . . like . . . my new . . . Am . . . air . . . ih . . . can . . . accent . . . ?

And the air base without foreground slightly inclined expounded 'a citation insulates moving thought wherever we reveal ourselves . . . pronounced the Name', and this does serve as some sort of baster . . . a consensus to thumb the arm signaling not here. No opinion here . . . to be having no need to drive a tusk into the versey and park it together there with the version shedding. In c̲itizenship a̲cross that c̲rest . . . or in k̲arma a̲cross that t̲ext . . . no opinion:

> First CAC, co-forsaken interpretation of the face. Simultaneous or not . . . the intention pulp . . . your name . . . my name . . . perverse for being mass

discounts. Discounts that the CAC co-builds the time perceived as our separation.

Next KAT, co-forcing without breath, you think the name explained or not . . . only your name . . . mine . . . the specialized name able even at the boundary of forward speech . . . to forget . . . to treat the echoes as points of comparison. The nation as omniscient house for the people's spirit . . . located in Cincinnati . . . with the haunting shade the obsession gave in the logic of its ghost/person exchange. No hurry . . . in no time . . . dream house . . . the accordion we are memory moves in.

This the latest flashbacks to be offered of our shared absence, and though it openly blots the study, it must not be assumed to have no theoretic point, no practical question . . . or archeological value. A dispossessed light in the last belonging of trauma before debt is the only eyewitness remaining. Note to self: once I followed my uncle (possibly David Antin?) in treating written language as predominantly spoken . . . and I inclined my ear to hear his mix . . . the tune was disrupted by my pronounced swallows, my elbow which grazed the tune indistinctly on the table I kept on hearing as 'canopy of the past'. Later on, when the post-operative unit had worn me out . . . the vision of my mother being helped as she sung 'the scars on neptune's surface' . . . and all this looks registered in my hand . . . the structure being only plans.

A gloss of the whole book to come has been . . . to pronounce the ancient but in deference to the ancient to not pronounce it distinctly. The usage report obviated wonder according to its writing understood as (capital 'I') idea the Name has substituted a course for . . . accidents waiting to avail themselves of method . . . begging to alter a different phase. I hope this doesn't sound culty, but the better exhibits are really on show inside the objects. They finally reduce the art of dressing risky to a last wish for your impossible future . . . like hose on the gravestone subliminal to the art of mourning photo . . . overworking the conspicuous growth of polarities . . . running on nothing but the gnostic claim for redacted unity it opposes. This arrangement, though previous, coincides with and classes the indecipherable interaction of the sublime and the line of gravestone® sandals for examples.

First of all, do not take the arranged perspective . . . since the diatribe's loose and sanctimonious assumptions and postulates were figured precise and preceptual . . . we've been trading in a transcendent though uninstructive dance of digressions . . . saying more and more frequently to every new sentence projected: . . . 'this sentence is also remarkable' . . . while the weight of suspiciously ripped angels hung in the important air thanks to antiquity enhancements. In any case, your location must be examined . . . your little red martyr got milked by crazy . . . so much for the author of our statement. Engulfing this curse thing are three imposed turning points . . . I won't call them reforms: (*a*) mention of the codeword (e.g. codeword *seaweed*, codeword *grand cyclops*); (*b*) secrecy . . . like 'make my folks forget my name' . . . and I wake at home into the consequent temporal difficulties (e.g. the *Home Alone* franchise); (*c*) the faux alien supremacy of our texts . . . signifying an unknown quantity of heterogenius masculine insertions at the appearance of any rule; and (d [or c^2]) given this anxious verist duty to suspend legislative operations by way of outnumbering, our observations of the law are mathematical . . . amounts to be the national voluntary reserve duty of our ancestors . . . and employ a combinatory homestead to approximately figure innovations as exceeding those old literary witnesses while replicating the ancestors' exilic entrance into a strange land (e.g. the text *kindles* desire) . . . (get it? *kindles*? like the electronic reader?). The order is d, c, and b . . . a is a given. The order is d, b, and a . . . no c. The order is b, c, d.

We may take for granted the removal of both meanings and the mundane in the no longer living corpus of the human idea (capital "I") . . . like some czar of old assumes the omission of carnal desire in his eunuch . . . so let's save our archeological zeal for a more watchable and punctuated missing . . . like let me just attach this to myself . . . and test it by avoiding unnecessary repetition over the course of this treatise . . . that that will appeal carefully to the scholar and layman alike, right? The story goes that a man can only be impregnated by a copyist's error . . . pulling out of presence before it's too late . . . I read this in a book and know it's true . . . the doctor said . . . dating has been around since the innovation of cause . . . hinting at some decline in the performance of methods for preventing loss . . . lamenting the lost art of visiting the sick . . . eloquently describing the transformative potential of incantation within the spiritual atmosphere of the feverish's delirium. He was refusing to acknowledge the most cogent reasons for discarding these practices, himself some disposed-of character whose refusal to reveal his desire as repetitious and unending . . . to see it as anything but innocuous and invisible to others . . . violently falsified an internal breadth of time . . . catalyzing the passing of event as before some basically racist ritual . . . the discriminated subjects are made to attentively prepare their bigot employers' attendance.

Let's turn now pretending to think in numbers, the premise being that language is a singularity in the second instance only . . . only allowing for a date of composition to date back to the appearance of an institution preceding it. Allegedly, it was once an alleged switchboard situated in the centre of an alleged cave set near the sea and it once allegedly directed the waters' current as though . . . in that doctor's reception room the glassed floating masks of us diagnoses-in-waiting were networked and chambered in the panels of a big screen control-room nearby. Captain Beefheart saying it over and over again . . . the largest living land mammal is the absent mind . . . the difference between a gymnast's and the TV broadcast's being . . . he can be either on either camera or in his hotel room . . . while the broadcast starts to fill each at a same. Critical updates keep membership by scrolling back to reason with the equipment malfunction. They are . . . the soul reillustrated to fill not only the whole legal body but its satellites of aura . . . jumping around with his ample bosom all but spilt out . . . apart from minor points . . . what must not be shown as public . . . anonymously on the verge of intention . . . in connexion with the prestigious text of the decade . . . finally a pleasurable questionnaire. We believe that this interaction cooked between yourself and the cultural moment was introduced in opposition to how it shifts . . . a conformity/non-conformity legend boarded under the misuse of naming the long struggle to reform.

Then, seeing that the whole unlimited company was

threatened, and that a great storm was redreaming the sky into flames and shite, we played that supplicatory roulette we had sworn against . . . and so poured out our hearts in prayer. A bronze flowerpot, sadly our last fascist souvenir, was tossed to the sea and the sea . . . charged by that hot-shot cattle prod . . . moved in a blurry gurgling manner, the way we wanted . . . towards the port. Fuck, how explicit do we need to be about this? It's all to test this great nation . . . to scaffold onto the announcer a terrifying confinement of the journey . . . we want you to find benefit in you . . . fire that cage, baby . . . pulse that den of lions in your chew . . . some of us here are creatures on that scaffold . . . mounting them strange shapes we thought was you . . . human friends . . . advancing the ceiling of our doubt . . . until the old usage of pronouncing the Name was then re-established. Weighty shadows of mire shown up as superfluous . . . meaningless . . . since they appear to have a similar meaning . . . please go away now . . . so it may be sufficient for our purposes to say they have unscrupulously forbidden (forgiven?) our attention in ordinary greetings . . . left the curation of the sentence as the substitute in any piece you take of your own writing for the reliable eye-witness of its information portability.

What reference text? The Name with the tune of amputation to past the body away . . . some trans-legalized time of skid row. According to the 1950s we not only paid off the existing debt by spilling the beans to random folk in the street . . . we also actually limited the correlation of cracks to the seconds counted . . . no sharing in the public registers because each instance is graphically isolated. To be lost in a crowd of consent both defective and a solution . . . tied together by the mentor of the previous saying . . . the outside sliding in context as object of communication. Not a secret too late to be in the least surrealist but listen adding is implicated in appearance . . . even if the thesis is missing . . . this need not be read as a denial of the circuit . . . it could be limited like this or this:

(*a*) it's not an ugly Name, it just assumes as necessary assumption that it knew the world before it was created . . . then rotates reference in the its

(*b*) there must be a good deal missing (a baby's act of thought is a constructing no-limit in space and time)

To hide among the public verses to prove this present context . . . is the neo-divide . . . entirely out of . . . place to think myself among the public as language . . . which means should a family member turn to me . . . even in the spirit of polytheism . . . even should they be the spouse I get laid with . . . and offer to me a cogent and noteworthy reason for just getting on with this . . . I am obliged to note . . . and to try and do so monstrously . . . and with emphatic stress . . . that loaded with the unforeseeable backsliding of our own conceptions . . . we must never get weary of repeating what we can not notice or know . . . repeating the gone banal oppositions of anarchive and archive . . . inconsequential spiritual unions repeated to fail at killing themselves off . . . with dubiously embedded reference to their implicated movement within their own accusations. Objection, right? Square brackets begin [that I borrowed the greeting phrase my friend would use as his distinctive calling card without permission and accordingly could discern a kind of minimum in any text . . . a truth that in truth's denial of context . . . just does not fit. The law, and here I apologize, deals more severely with the thief than with the robber. To my ear, this is because if we ever found the way the technical angle leaks out to more than function . . . we would kill it . . . it's why we can't really know our times or minutes . . . can only account for them with reference.

But don't get old on your mum now . . . sure this doesn't pronounce the Name per se . . . but it does roll out the following three stages as summary: (1) after you got isolated in the good old times . . . you denied the continuation of the Name under public scrutiny; (2) a morning later in the time when I finally reversed the customs . . . office to re-establish the look they gave each other reflected in the description of the symbolic as it; (3) with an establishment of desire in the works . . . a line was drawn between coerced error and mistake . . . between the body as temple and the body as outside, so (3) when I rudely . . . like some invertebrate breather pointed out man-boobs in the oeuvre the pronunciation endlessly begins to list all that shit rising up as covered in the same way. We can't agree to this, right . . . but it is preferable to bone reconstruction . . . whose praxis is necessary only to reform the minimal lisp of this text's thing . . . doubtless . . . to intern anew an expertise in pairing soda and solid at the Name's obscure report.

Their right to soldier on so that the custom knows what's what . . . first corroboration's the echoiest . . . first corroboration good fade . . . first corroborated then altered in some other night . . . shadow first you second degree valentine. A weighting objection to the dismissal . . . bowled anon . . . caught anon . . . what appeal shouts . . . replaying the digital analysis for its precise verb . . . New York is for real you don't have to ask.

Ok, let's confirm the order . . . you boarded a bus to Philly at 1:15 under the Name . . . Morve Beenborg . . . wrote 'dister alist likey' in your notebook . . . you went to the sixth floor of the medical counsel . . . you uttered . . . in a low voice . . . an otherwise ingenious hypothesis about the coring of the Name . . . fact it was impossible to pronounce in accordance with its writing . . . and then what?

If this was stopped . . . who was co-staging the people's response and . . . what was the point of handing out leftovers if they couldn't be heard at all? Shaking hand was the reason for this surname, still, was it not more likely the dorky confusion of crediting yourself with prophetic powers? Sick of the arching shank bone that marks the final stage . . . I am quite free to counteract the erudite barrier of history with any old shit that has survived . . . limited, of course, to the insurmountable afterbirths of a day's duration. This is so done already . . . but I am probably not trying to find a key for some riddle of gates . . . and for a good many reasons . . . and from a simple driving into of dissection . . . and sloping out of the worst observations stuffed with the home sensor . . . theories as permissive as the older ones in encouraging themselves their own contribution . . . absorbing the train-a-coming or wash behind our ears like a sanity . . . and not even our own undoubted antipathy for ourselves could relieve us or them of it.

Yet I want to know . . . the matter seems so simple. Other people are in the writing as Names on the proposition of movement. The author lived in an age and country where both pronunciation and illiteracy were codeterminously forbidden. It is exactly the time that your translator must have lived in the same country and period and has brought this with them from

their native land. They have something to do with themselves
. . . yet can't get over the difficulty that there was a time when
pronunciation was strictly forbidden . . . this took place as sold
in the near future. Using supernatural states of tone . . . but with
a degree of that ephemeral tact which so many of us lack . . .
she mockingly released herself from prison, went to the royal
palace, and whispered the Name itself into the terrified King's
ear . . . then inscribed the Name on a King's ear-shaped tablet
and gave it to him. Whatever the King had thought was great
writing died in blasphemy that day to a deeper place too easily
local and judged only by need. Whatever . . . I try whispering
. . . but it doesn't sound the same . . . it shakes my head as
a transcribed witness's testimony struck from the environment
and time I reflect when I put forward this earnest negation of
those who repressed it . . . of substance and removal . . . I have
this to say . . . the joke is on . . . who . . . poetry arriving as
though a farce/force . . . field open . . . it's that knowing that
. . . force/farce . . . you see coming from any direction. Reading
Frank for sexual admission . . . this text . . . shuddering asshole
in the cold . . . of old . . . age . . . this text . . . as the radar will
raid . . . not quite as destitute as we were . . . in 1334, my love,
my love . . . this text, as re-established above . . . confirms this.

II.
Visibility

An arrhythmia of uncertain age and origin served as a countenance . . . a pure lamp of lightening . . . was actually yes . . . an angle . . . forced in the eschatological age upon the biology of vision. Not true there is only one clue . . . I made the dream-text without doing shit. And the worst violence is to be made visible . . . so I keep one part suddenly compiled by its earlier anonymous one. Thus the term used for seeing in here is conversational spreading down the sight of a string to the light of a fuller treatment than can be accorded here. It's really never equal to a false home and is not a place to re-treat what repeats to transform its departure. Even so . . . nerving the less . . . mobile chance . . . to look at where it twists . . . still worth bobbing here . . . in some parts of the water.

As to the origin of this boat on the bus off track, it really is anthropology . . . just studying the presupposed invisibility of the observer to death as a countenance of resonating bright confusion. To make this point clearer . . . if the writing weren't asked to cover itself as though that were its truth . . . it would cease to be acknowledged a virtuality we might live for. Dismantle a peroration of the machine so learning how. Or should another version of this world, owing to our errors, depart just like that as the midst of our prophetic vision?

With my Pop watching fake son while I play upon the Wii . . . burning down here in the juice we have elaborated . . . I was experienced by the Lord as a revelation to Him . . . I was a fork that He must chew . . . chew . . . choose from three diverging paths . . . this into that or abandoned to form a launch like pad for the grand opening bash of apocalyptic utterances. Like birds on a mention now we see through a mirror that in the future we will see eye to eye . . . incarnate . . . since we have relegated school to the future world as a dialogue between surprise and resemblance. On the very spot that I write 'that rickety bench that rickety bench' I cannot read the impression it made and I deny it ever . . . that God would make His final form visible to a fully tenured faculty eye of the rational that blinked just once to dream of a great theophany . . . then opened eye to eye to some Robocop daiquiri just nixed in a lovey disc . . . self-portrait entitled 'narc as bird' visible across the store . . . a clash in the car tint to enclose contact . . . spine of the Book of Jubilees too little to toast . . . and then blindly spread sunscreen on . . . fascinated by circles on the tin man's face in the song so fat with surface.

Them ruins are covert paws . . . as if . . . steeped for signing . . . they grew . . . attaching special meaning to the audience of this thought . . . a more intimate relation of touch to speech than our historical knowledge can explain or warrant. Note why the touch is visible as not quite a bearing when pointed to repeatedly point from the unmistakable vibrancy around your messed up hair. When I can't respond or commune with desire . . . cause so flipped . . . so weighed down with pride . . . it's discernible only to the *idea* of my mind . . . whose action is raised by a stream of apologetics so lacking in pitch relation . . . it mistakes these cardboard forceps for the starting point of meaningful code. Languages that reread the friends we don't yet . . . or are waiting to friend . . . to discover that all departing mentalities when taking leave of their introductions apply the waiting on a scale to be . . . which . . . theorizes the origin of meaning.

This touch like speech we're following is something even more reductive than saying it's outside music . . . an exercise that beats you up until you grow up . . . fills the modern youth with the strength to never deserve their former validations. Struck dead on draft night and still you say the ministering angels of death cannot see God, who like a sports metaphor imagines it picks you. Say it again . . . no more metaphors . . . but the evil reports on purity and impurity keep on circulating in the movie industry's underworld as the underworlds keep on trucking in the movies metaphorically as concealed systems of power within community that threaten to chasm an individual's relation to the law . . . thus sayeth the vigilante . . . a law unto themself.

There are: the scoffers, the hypocrites, the scorners . . . evil reports blazing over wooded backyards to make that comfort real. Here's how I like to begin: in a series of secret homebases scattered to thin my moral shortcomings to the fringes of transference . . . and though I particularly no longer permit myself to ball-bounce (a metaphorically constructed sports-playing with psychologically transparent leagues and players) . . . and while I have particularly neglected the practice of predicting deaths of little children as a deterrent from sexual aberration . . . I continue to observe R.D.'s permission to return to a spasmodic folk-tale meadow of the no soap radio legend.

This very same mode induced my friend to ask: why is training always repetition? Good question, right? I shutteth my eyes . . . genuinely looking to see far off into the opposite direction from where the food goes in continuation. And though it was prohibited to stare . . . he was just a half-naked twig repeating laundry for the lunacy it admits. The terrifying consortium of abstinence and the smell of the globe . . . to mend the climate by offering it a gift . . . as though the performance weight of healing was root crusted through charity and lovingkindness. Andrew formulates the stale doctrine this way: he says Lord to the photon . . . blows his glass for religious object (a food bong) . . . a mental patient slash organ donor privately offers some gift to a King . . . it is altogether doubtful whether it will be accepted . . . he or she then undergoes this diversion . . . that even should the ruler accept the gift . . . their wish to meet the giver remains far from certain . . . this patient donor slash mental organ then gets obsessed with being received by the King . . . and adorns him or her self with all the dashed up subjecthood he or she can stand . . . that's the end of the story and the end of the story is that its moral application intimates that it might be of great merit to your conception of your deeds and actions in this world.

To partake in the great future revolution . . . to shape a churn's goop . . . all flesh consumed without discrimination . . . reads into Han Solo's stride . . . a ghostly spanner to service motes . . . when we awake we will be recorded into the complex mess falling from aborted heights. The very tissue of the season seems . . . based on a previous occasion we recall . . . to have performed poorly . . . ends offer on quoted stock . . . projected up on the moon with His finger . . . but you can't start yet . . . you are winning. To hire some arm . . . a warp grows persecuted as usual . . . a silent phobia wake-a-thon in the mouth of you your client . . . where we sleep. I seek to be paid . . . at regular intervals . . . a paid visit to visit you my friend . . . so I stay in grad school . . . and here I am accomplice from applying my witness of this alarm . . . that the upper ones are sustained by the splendor of the holy spirit while the lower ones if they do not toil will starve.

Before concluding this section I am part myself both before at after. The beauty of the lining of any throat is that it puts on lines in an air of speech. Graces . . . each geography . . . was once before famous . . . as a great beauty in the muddle of consequence. In other words . . . all who partook in this Midwestern town's joyful suppression of the apocalyptists . . . sitting around with crowns on their strands . . . drinking the few remaining strands of relation to see the manner of their placing in one last line before the open tomb. Real apprehensive like . . . this open tune in sonar . . . its play some weird accomplice to steeping form before you pour . . . camp counselor mounts his pop-arts little deuce coupe slash . . . boogie nights style . . . you don't know what I got. Would like a look from us to recoil into wicked people are charitable too . . . invisible merits attaining a nearness to poor visibility . . . pulled over . . . breathing guilt into the realizer.

III.

Memoir

This picture stuck on septic . . . dictated by a range of violations to the impressive corrosions of stopped-up filial piety. It's a lotto narrated by three main aims or some other number to approximate chance of exactitude. To freshen that welsh rarebit cranked through the memory math after failure to try the door. To descend in my issued state to the impression-moment of forced constraints as necessarily the imposition of subject . . . and fault the descriptive view taken. Finally, in view of the utilitarian construction of the rec room that prevails in our time . . . to air a sheet or mattress there . . . and then lucidly dance the religious ancestral dance of sycophancy to that higher being . . . a joy insured by feeling the issue of death . . . landing after life on the larvae bib propped around the abandoned shale-mining site . . . too late not to be. I have the advantage here of drawing freely from the top 50 miss charts of my parents' youth . . . turds now to attention to command the biographical anti-manicure . . . stigmatizing each of two different readings of dogging at school.

Summer after summer, our choice on the platter . . . travel nuggets . . . exhaustive but entertaining. A particularly fascinating excess wall of sleep . . . wall of lickable writing . . . its deed in the never not being read called resting . . . the means within. We stood up in the boat opposite to the wet bear . . . five baby bears on it . . . with all the means of our power of undivided community . . . urging everyone to do the wave . . . quietly . . . to understand the specks of water oscillating in the fans of the light expected at any moment. I place a mojo to my ear . . . this doesn't need to be proven to me to be . . . if you wear the national outfit you . . . you just end up making patriotic speeches.

Like a tax-collector who works only the underground places . . . just listen to all the accounts . . . to the way talking seeps in or out . . . fashioning the guide for our confirmation class . . . consciousness or what. And I will gain the devotion of all who know bullshit to be bad . . . trespass on the allotted toner . . . shake it to milk it . . . and make friends easily and keep them, right? Like so many planetary projections . . . arrested by their own alignments of birth . . . first-born coming into the world as variability . . . they founded by signature . . . like eyelids . . . they found it difficult to not believe they had been away . . . distracted but working on the preposal . . . impossible to detect or expose . . . that what hasn't happened is a translation . . . what has is lost. Just heard this . . . but indignantly refused the request.

Most of her views were much older than her . . . split the biro to make broad strokes . . . but the gates to this distance were imperceptible . . . a treated distance telling the plot to be revised . . . foundational but definitely not waving. She had arrived all ready . . . appropriating when she arrived . . . her vast feat at the gymnasium . . . exposed while changing . . . suitable confessions of her various mistakes conceived as inside so to be recited from memory . . . advantageous to her inseparable columns of codes and friends. I really want to go away from home for college . . . she in one of our dawn sessions . . . turning left . . . a hundred theatrical figures of perspectives . . . specializing in the cuneiform of apparent ease. Then . . . here's how to make your way through a text from cover to cover: go to political meetings; meet the leading intellectuals of your day; read thousands of novels, make marginal notes; receive a research grant to spend a year just wondering from library to library; fill notebooks with transcriptions of experience; cultivate a working knowledge of at least ten languages. This is not the opinion of any single ordinary person but was compiled through a survey of the career backgrounds of literati and the otherwise culturally elite.

Untrammelled by the soul-destroying and irksome parts of contemporary living, I like to organically garden the recurrent forms as they pop up in the organized presence of metaphor. Emancipated by the simultaneous arousal in this research . . . finding that any two things are the same. Volume beyond our comprehension . . . in fracture and network . . . the rooms wiped out from our minds guarantee the silent processes of history. Chaotic point followed by a coded leap . . . used up to be opened for laid aside only . . . the profound liturgical impressionism of the concordance's vaunted light. If a thought . . . cast enthusiastically to end with cash . . . gilt-edging the psychologist's office at the far end of Terminal D . . . saying: if the terminal map were the only achievement of aviation . . . and was all that was rediscovered after cellular devolution . . . it would be sufficient to justify our civilization's existence. This is an oversight but remains. Picabia writes but only money has genius. What is . . . all the available material on the dogmas of our nation? Let's see how much we bid. Well, it's proof that we got onto the panel . . . and I just take delight in proving any system of arrangement in writing . . . now, let's get into the back of a germ and publish it again for the first time . . . in the critical edition . . . this is not officially over. She then completed a number of interesting studies on folk-lore poems motivated by both inevitability and slight inappropriateness.

She contributed to scholarship on the manuscripts of the Renaissance obscurantist Steinschneider, who wrote only in light and maintained the alterior principle that there was never time isolated from an exterior world . . . rather it is a fence fully beyond us that traces an interplay it is necessarily blind to.

So much for the blind variant which makes fun of a baby . . . to its Name nonetheless . . . the problem . . . keeps a treasury of potential disease . . . keeps on with being like . . . anything more or less complex . . . she receives through the epigenetic expression of her nations' language. So, however moral the influence . . . those value motifs that counsel your intentions . . . if we start with the effect of the right upon the judge . . . we must go back to writing prophecies . . . however surprising and improbable they may seem. To question why is such a destiny . . . foreseen in a fate far worse than reason. Calamity painted chemically on the shocking holy saint . . . no alternatives tiding to this most pessimistic light. Again, this is the wavering rendered by perception as privileged site of experiment . . . the finger's excursive wagging . . . so I'm inclined to throw out the word triclinium here . . . one which were we privy enough to enter . . . we'd notice a tasteful little puke trough against the left-hand wall . . . to even be described as a rationalist here . . . here right at the base of furnishing this puke séance smell . . . is to encourage visions of the original bad guy of the darkest times. A descriptive syntax of discontinuity? Well, that's just a further deifying of the individual . . . did they really remove the foreskin to bare the pain of foresight . . . to prepare, hygienically, the victims of future thoughts? Then I felt our transcendence echo fluid upon a method all shades of belief and un-belief . . . equal footing of too much firmness . . . by which the telegraphy antenna was once due its first wireless song . . . tapped out your co-operation as defense of dogma . . . and we left her amplified in subterfuge . . . attempting to hide her research . . . you know what I felt then? (I had begun with a question) . . . sectarian resentment, friend . . . to ward off the entropic excesses of experience . . . sectarian boundaries.

The bulk of repentance is for rethinking youth . . . something determined to be a choice to move away from . . . talents understood to be clustering at the messes to move towards. I therefore choose the language according to a theme of imagining thinking . . . as though once asleep . . . always asleep . . . since sleep cannot verify what was waking . . . we dream the residual sense-impressions as arising in the article that precedes them. Isn't our own minds a kind of scarecrow here . . . insects formed only when they have just entered the tent . . . to limit our knowledge of some accession to power (potentially fascist) . . . this examination, shame and all, limited to imagining this. Exit the promise of (capital "I") imagination (I am thinking here of the American Modernist poets who stayed in America) . . . having constructed a working hostility . . . resistance repeated in bitter disappointment as boundary . . . rather than the already reoccurring condition of a sub-linguistic syntax pulse and its historicity (à la Lezama Lima). This is the kind of equivocal wisdom we just can't not answer back to . . . pleading to our publishers that they never stop deleting our Names as founding editors of this series. It's the same inferiority uncertainty of a joint re-consideration that attracts our magical performances addiction to public utterance.

There are: the dilettantes, the popularizers, the resenters, pretenders . . . and due to the familial pleasures they derive in their bias against laypersons . . . they actually have the hardest time imperfecting their work. Eating peaches off some terribly pat trees . . . they choose the most expressive words to neatly riddle who is 'really' alive . . . and I contribute with the strength of my antipathies, dislikings, and weaknesses . . . but I might presuppose to have my theories about that. Like some ongoing prejudice stuck me as an observer . . . what does one do with that? After all, we don't vacuum in a vacuum. To change places with that, qualify it . . . she would warm up her pupils by looking out . . . to voice the question: why do we even want to find a way to represent the natural . . . changing this occasionally to nautical . . . (then going under . . . our bodies are disemvoiced in the water) . . . our voices are disembodied . . . she says . . . witness the room . . . to throw some light. I wish to lower the standards of original work required by learned institutions . . . express thanks rushing to their failure to acknowledge the wobble required for climactivity (to quote A.L.G. Jr.) . . . the great drawback they make room for . . . to probingly hinder any not super-material thoughts about the term progress. But an instance comes to my geographical location . . . approaching screen . . . in the constellations I am forming . . . refusing to absorb the pace of sacred undertaking . . . a cold rejoinder comes to mind . . . refusing to assimilate the memory of the given unit of this . . . no indexical aids and therefore no abstraction . . . throws the malice in it to compromise . . . to be exposed as training for this prodigious adversary . . . spoken shadow set up as the law.

It was a signpost on the crossroads in the valley of the shadow of death but what counted for attention was recognition . . . whereas we referenced each other by either seriousness, jokes, or some combination (where still the comic was either ascendant or subordinate). So we may miss the sign with positive enthusiasm . . . excited by the incomprehensible fluke . . . and with no reservations about logical inconsistencies in the continuous truth convictions of the continuous book. Possible idea flux shaking fork in the times . . . subtitle blind points equilibrium . . . according the garb it appears as its form. Hypothesis to own words minus valued warning . . . it's whatever never ceases . . . leads to the propagation of value through dialectic of advancement and scrutiny . . . the past in foundational all . . . party and present to the bound to . . . undermining a new slogan for pacifism . . . no . . . it is oppose no one's opposition. Don't get me here . . . I love the stamina of numbering as much as any plan loves its economy . . . but between the Keebler elves emblem and the artificial soil . . . and me seasoned to guard the award everywhere of exile . . . I'm drowsy omniscient right now . . . heaps of foretelling but no daring, see . . . the precincts work to prevent access to yonder research chambers . . . and the object is to uproot the good historical reasoning that is undisturbed as fact . . . but with such competing words as power paws . . . it's too much storm for the near futile mind. Instead, we boast an adhering reader into conveyance . . . disperse just enough authority as to readily and freely fondle the creator. Serious question: is this a serious disagreement at the house of mourning . . . or just some domestic encouragement machine of materialism and apathy . . . rich in its lack of proper parable?

Born primigeniously and without warning this audience-clad figure has a formidable honing instinct housed on its side in a cone-shaped organ which mid-flight turns aloud right up the sacred scroll . . . uh . . . uh . . . uh . . . what is a kind of bird that is amazing? Or there was a deepening warning we neglected . . . our little doors gone haywire . . . because the end is always characteristic. Depth of feeling departing from the atmosphere of letters in the very movie of origin . . . which may or may not have been . . . like the welfare widow may have lacked the memorized civic nous . . . yet without compliance notes . . . before the trustees of the Centre for the Disestablished . . . lines to singe a bill. But that's how we heretics do . . . at the visiting hours of this ancestral midriff . . . achingly poor . . . and gone . . . but we still visit . . . to follow for discounted aid their example . . . muttering Osirian blues . . . semi-circles signing more than sound on our synonyms . . . walking in the footsteps of the footsteps of the footsteps of their four Virgilesque bears for spirit guides.

More junk than the picture should emerge . . . conversation with an unhinge searching hints of pathology for the fringe she's absorbed in. Group-like . . . intention freed by interconnected expansion rather than erasure of the author. . . . in the dignified condescension of any instance of any mission . . . the speech, she admits, may have been counterfeit, but the infinitesimal tears were really real. I want to encourage research and raise the standards of scholarly practice to a really high level . . . here's to hoping we can reverse human aging and finally taste the crisp figment of heaven . . . we'll all be articulate ministers . . . that is, recognized authoritative spokespeople of our age. But the meek who are also really funny . . . a gutsy bunch who might just inherit the earth . . . or keep some hard and bitter shadow of it . . . will modestly yet wryly say they saw that coming . . . the impetuous grafting onto a spindle of energy . . . but from the limits of the stage the limits of monadic self . . . parent-teacher meetings if you know what I mean . . . not to take away the com[m]a of my own responsibility of course.

Wrapped in the wrecked but half-obscured circles of interpretation . . . there is a kind of double-vertigo to struggle with . . . a strange reproductive move to reproduce the move as somehow not memory. Fervent insistence to know the carry-on as it walks . . . or before we illicitly consume it. The flower pulpit I feel so intolerant of is the spiritual legacy of their latinate Names . . . latinate Names, modes of transportation that make the generally stupid reign of the idea of the world as presiding over the circle it floats in . . . well . . . worth living. The quit then answers only as long as the interruption fostered in its supply . . . to think of a void . . . then think of a word . . . like Wall St. . . . and watch it float there . . . the inferno of our spiritual legacy.

ACKNOWLEDGEMENTS

TRANSGRESSION is, I think, in line with its contrarian impulse—the product and labour of continuance—and is hardly without, in fact necessarily bears, its own systems of fidelities and respects. It is my hope that my family, both dead and living, despite what might be to them potentially unrecognizable forms of continuance at work in this work, might believe me when I write that the trangressions that compose this book do not comprise a fantasy of escape, but on the contrary, a fantasy (perhaps of equal delusion) of inescapable continuity everywhere. I offer a real thanks to my family, both dead and living, for the privilege of being granted such a legible archive, and a special thanks to the vexed debts of my maternal patrilineage which have so utterly haunted the impossible question-events of self-relation for me.

IMPOSSIBLY large thank yous are owed to the stunning intelligence and generosity of so many friends who have helped in the process of this book by taking the time to read from it, and/or offer comments and encouragement, and/or publish and circulate it (if I forgot anyone, please know it was only during the moments of list-making): David Brazil, Brandon Brown, Macgregor Card, Corina Copp, Ted Dodson, Jordan Dunn, Megan Ewing, Thomas Fink, Norman Finkelstein, Glen Frieden, Judith Goldman, Whit Griffin, Roberto Harrison, Andrew Hladky, Seth Landman, Susan Landers, Jess Mynes, Jennifer Nelson, Emily Pettit, Zack Pieper, Judah Rubin, Lauren Russell, Karl Saffran, Ian Sansom, Wayne Stables, Scott Thurston, Anna Vitale, Cathy Wagner, Dana Ward, Nathaniel Weaver, Tyrone

Williams, Matvei Yankelevich, and Joey Yearous-Algozin. A special thanks to Andy Gricevich, whose careful readings of and innumerable conversations about this book have deeply shaped the dimensions of my relation to it. I am deeply grateful to Daniel Owen for tirelessly advocating for and investing in this text and for his patient and always useful editorial insight (and by extension a huge thanks to Ugly Duckling Presse). Finally, an inestimable thanks to Lisa Hollenbach for what so often feels like everything to me.

SELECTIONS from this book have been published in *6x6*, *Cannot Exist*, *Divine Magnet*, *Epiphany*, *Everyday Genius*, *Graven Images*, *Jubilat*, *The Other Room Anthology*, *Plumberries*, *Poems by Sunday*, *Private Line*, and *Well Greased*.

THE epigraph by Gershom Scholem is excerpted from his article 'The Name of God and the Linguistic Theory of Kabbala (Part 2)', translated by Simon Pleasance, and appearing in *Diogenes* 80 (1972).